BRITISH STEAM LOCOMOTIVES
BEFORE PRESERVATION

A Study of Before and Afterlife

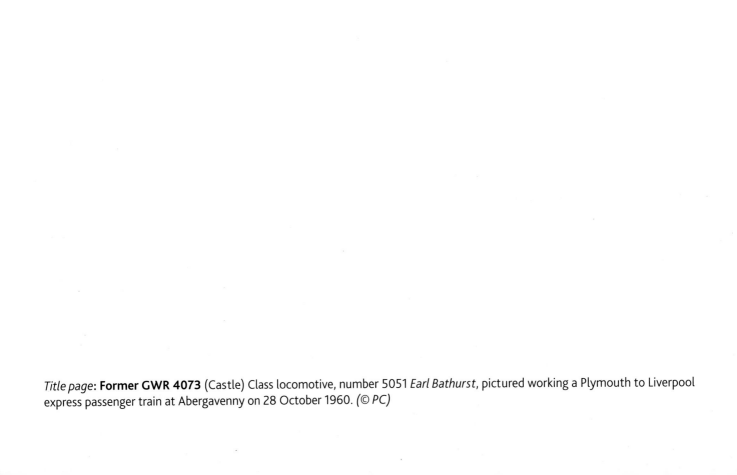

Title page: **Former GWR 4073** (Castle) Class locomotive, number 5051 *Earl Bathurst*, pictured working a Plymouth to Liverpool express passenger train at Abergavenny on 28 October 1960. *(© PC)*

BRITISH STEAM LOCOMOTIVES
BEFORE PRESERVATION

A STUDY OF BEFORE AND AFTERLIFE

MALCOLM CLEGG

PEN & SWORD
TRANSPORT

AN IMPRINT OF PEN & SWORD BOOKS LTD.
YORKSHIRE – PHILADELPHIA

First published in Great Britain in 2020 by
Pen and Sword Transport
An imprint of
Pen & Sword Books Ltd
Yorkshire - Philadelphia

ISBN 978 1 52676 046 3

Typeset by Aura Technology and Software Services, India.
Printed and bound by Printworks Global Ltd, London/Hong Kong

Pen & Sword Books Ltd incorporates the Imprints of Pen & Sword Books Archaeology, Atlas, Aviation, Battleground, Discovery, Family History, History, Maritime, Military, Naval, Politics, Railways, Select, Transport, True Crime, Fiction, Frontline Books, Leo Cooper, Praetorian Press, Seaforth Publishing, Wharncliffe and White Owl.

For a complete list of Pen & Sword titles please contact

PEN & SWORD BOOKS LIMITED
47 Church Street, Barnsley, South Yorkshire, S70 2AS, England
E-mail: enquiries@pen-and-sword.co.uk
Website: www.pen-and-sword.co.uk

or

PEN AND SWORD BOOKS
1950 Lawrence Rd, Havertown, PA 19083, USA
E-mail: Uspen-and-sword@casematepublishers.com
Website: www.penandswordbooks.com

CONTENTS

ACKNOWLEDGEMENT

I would like to offer my sincere thanks and appreciation to Mr Peter Cookson for allowing the publication of photographs from his private collection in this book.

Credits and Copyright

As is often the case with photographic collections, exchanges between collectors and the acquisition of other collections sometimes makes it impossible to credit the original photographer with a particular picture. There are also occasions when the same basic picture is taken by different photographers, especially on works and locomotive shed visits. For these reasons, the illustrations appearing in this book are simply credited to the Peter Cookson Collection (marked PC), © Peter Cookson, or to the Author's Collection (marked MC), © Malcolm Clegg.

INTRODUCTION

The practice of preserving steam locomotives in Britain dates back more than 150 years.

The world's oldest preserved steam locomotive is the *Puffing Billy,* which was designed and built by William Hedley, a British industrial engineer and Overseer (manager) of the Wylam Colliery near Newcastle-Upon-Tyne in County Durham. He was assisted in the building project by the colliery blacksmith Timothy Hackworth. *Puffing Billy* was introduced into service in 1813 to haul fully laden coal wagons a distance of some eight miles from Wylam Colliery to the docks at Lemington-on-Tyne, relying on the power of the steam locomotive together with the adhesion and strength of iron wheels on iron rails. The locomotive was a huge success and continued to operate for almost half a century before being withdrawn from service in 1862. The locomotive was later transported to London on loan to the Patent Office Museum, which became a part of the London Science Museum in 1883 (later renamed the Kensington Science Museum).

Puffing Billy was later sold to the museum for £200 and displayed there until it was moved to the National Railway Museum (NRM) at York, where it is currently on display. Two replicas of *Puffing Billy* are in existence. One, which was built in 1906, is on display in the Deutsches Museum in Munich, Germany, and the other, built in 2005, is in the Beamish Museum in County Durham.

Stephenson's original *Rocket* locomotive was also donated to the Patent Office Museum in 1862 and later exhibited at the Kensington Science Museum until 2018, when it was loaned to the Museum of Science & Industry in Manchester.

In September 2019, *Rocket* was put on public display at the NRM in York on a long term loan. She is expected to remain there for at least ten years, after which, her future will be reviewed. Another nineteenth century preserved steam locomotive which is on popular display at the Kensington Science Museum in London, is steam locomotive number 49 *Columbine* which was built at Crewe in 1845 for the Grand Junction Railway Company. This locomotive is likely to remain in the Science Museum for the foreseeable future.

The original *Rocket* locomotive referred to above, has gone through several modifications since first appearing at the Rainhill Trials in 1830. However, a replica of the *Rocket* as it first appeared in 1830 can also be seen at the National Railway Museum in York, and a second 1830 replica is exhibited at the German National Transport Museum located in Nuremburg.

The success of the *Puffing Billy* in 1813 was instrumental in William Hedley building a sister locomotive, the *Wylam Dilly,* which was introduced in 1815. This locomotive also had a working life span of almost fifty years, operating at the Wylam Colliery until 1862 and then at the Craghead Colliery near Stanley in County Durham. After being withdrawn from service, the *Wylam Dilly* was also preserved, after being presented to the Royal Museum in Edinburgh which later became the National Museum of Scotland. The *Wylam Dilly* is the second oldest surviving steam locomotive in the world, after its sister locomotive *Puffing Billy.*

As the nineteenth century progressed, railway companies became aware of the importance of preserving their history and they were inspired by the opening of the world's first National Railway Museum at Hamar, Norway, in 1896, followed by the German National Railway Museum at Nuremburg in 1899.

Although discussions were held in Britain and railway companies started storing artefacts and material with a view to preserving their heritage, no concerted effort was made to actually establish a national railway museum, although some items were put on public display at various railway stations. Lack of space was often problematic for storing large items such as locomotives. The Great Western Railway (GWR) for example stored two locomotives, *North Star* and *Lord of the Isles*, at Swindon Works in order that they may be preserved. Unfortunately, the space occupied by the locomotives was later required for other purposes deemed more important, and in 1906 both locomotives were cut up for scrap.

It was the London and North Eastern Railway Company (LNER) which was at the forefront of the campaign to preserve railway history in Britain and in 1927 the company opened Britain's first public railway museum, the LNER Museum in Queen Street, York.

By the latter part of the 1930s, all of the big four railway companies had amassed a significant amount of railway memorabilia. Other private institutions such as the Stephenson Locomotive Society (established in 1909) also had significant collections. The LNER Railway Museum kindly allowed substantial amounts of material from these sources to be exhibited at their York museum, but as the outbreak of the Second World War drew ever closer, all prospects of creating a national railway museum rapidly declined.

After the war years, the prospect of establishing a national railway museum was back on the agenda and the nationalisation of the railways in 1948 presented an ideal opportunity for the nation's collection of railway memorabilia to be brought together for the first time. Various discussions took place and a decision was reached to expand the LNER Museum at York to include additional

materials from other sources. The changes which followed eventually led to the formation of the National Railway Museum at Leeman Road in York, which today houses many of the nation's railway artefacts and memorabilia as well as being the home of numerous preserved steam locomotives from all over the country and other parts of the world.

It is recognised that the big four railway companies that existed from 1923 until 1948 also played a vital role in preserving locomotives and other railway memorabilia, and after the railways were nationalised in 1948, the British Transport Commission and later British Railways (BR) continued to make significant contributions by continuing to preserve railway artefacts.

During the early 1960s, as the steam era came to an end, the railway authorities agreed to preserve a considerable number of additional steam locomotives for posterity as a part of the 'National Collection'. These locomotives were restored to their former glory and are now an important part of the nation's railway heritage under ownership of the National Railway Museum in York. The museum displays a collection of over 100 locomotives and is the largest and busiest railway museum in the world, attracting almost a million visitors each year.

That, however, was not the end of the line in the quest to preserve steam locomotives. Two major decisions were taken between 1959 and 1963 by the British Government which led to the introduction of numerous heritage railways and a significant number of additional steam locomotives being preserved.

In 1959, it was announced that all steam power would be withdrawn from the railways within the next decade to prevent an uneconomical two-tier system of steam and diesel (excluding electric) motive power operating side by side for the life expectancy of steam engines still being built. This resulted in a hasty demise of steam locomotives during the early 1960s, which gave rise to vast numbers becoming readily available for purchase at affordable scrap prices.

In excess of 13,000 steam locomotives were withdrawn from service between 1960 and the end of steam in 1968. Apart from those which British Railways had agreed to preserve, these locomotives in the main were scrapped by BR or were sold to numerous scrap metal merchants to be cut up and disposed of in private scrap yards.

The second major change was announced in 1963 when the Beeching Report (*The Reshaping of British Railways*) was published, which recommended the closure of over 5,000 miles of track and 2,363 railway stations on the railway network in Britain. The report was accepted by the government and the majority of the changes were implemented.

Opposition to these drastic changes led to the formation of numerous protest groups, as well as preservation societies and groups of individuals who made concerted efforts to purchase and preserve branch lines which had been closed, or were earmarked for closure. Considerable success was achieved by their efforts, hard work and dedication, which resulted in numerous branch lines and other stretches of railway lines being saved after being purchased from British Railways for private use.

In order to operate these heritage railways, a considerable amount of rolling stock was required and steam traction seemed ideally suited for this purpose. The public at large were captivated by old railway steam locomotives and large numbers were now available at scrap prices resulting from the rapid withdrawal of steam which was taking place at the time.

Operators of the newly formed heritage railways, together with preservation groups, made every effort to purchase as many of these steam locomotives as possible in the time they were available. Consequently, hundreds of steam locomotives were either bought directly from BR or, more commonly, purchased from scrap metal dealers before they were cut up and disposed of. Their subsequent introduction onto private heritage railways proved to be a very popular choice.

Disposal of condemned steam locomotives

Prior to 1959, all British Railways-owned locomotives that had been withdrawn from service and condemned were cut up and disposed of within the railway organisation itself. The policy changed in 1959 in order to cope with the anticipated increase in the numbers of steam locomotives expected to be withdrawn from service over the next few years. This followed the announcement that all steam locomotives would be withdrawn from the railway network as quickly as possible and replaced by diesel and electric forms of traction by 1969.

It was decided that a number of reputable private scrap metal merchants, nationwide, would be selected and allowed to purchase condemned locomotives from BR. They would be responsible for cutting up and dismantling the locomotives for disposal as scrap metal. The scheme was closely monitored and a number of conditions were imposed upon the scrap dealers. Some of these conditions involved the resale of locomotives to third parties such as private individuals and preservation groups.

In 1959, the first private scrap merchant to purchase steam locomotives from BR was a firm called Woodham Brothers Ltd of Barry in South Wales. This was a long established family business that began trading in 1892 as Woodham & Sons. In 1959, the firm was owned and run by Mr Dai Woodham. His elder brother, Albert Woodham, a former co-owner, had retired from the business several years earlier. Woodham Brothers had in the past disposed of other forms of scrap materials which they had purchased under contract from BR and were already in the process of cutting up large numbers of condemned coal wagons which they had been purchasing from BR under contract since 1957. There appeared to be an almost unlimited supply of these condemned coal wagons as BR had decided in 1955 to scrap over 600,000 of them, surplus to requirements due to the decline of the coal industry in Britain.

In the spring of 1959, Dai Woodham spent a week at Swindon Railway Works where he was taught the methods used by BR to dismantle and scrap steam locomotives. In March of that year the first of many locomotives began to arrive at his scrapyard, which was situated on a disused section of Barry Docks. His premises were leased from the British Transport Docks Board and located adjacent to a large number of railway sidings which he was also able to lease. These sidings had in the past formed part of a marshalling yard for coal wagons used during the heyday of shipping Welsh coal from the former South Wales Coalfield through the port of Barry. The sidings were ideal for Dai Woodham to stable the steam locomotives and coal wagons which he had purchased from BR until they could be cut up and disposed of.

In the summer of 1959, Woodham Brothers employees began cutting up steam locomotives which the firm had purchased from BR. Dai Woodham quickly realised however that it was far quicker, easier and more lucrative to concentrate on scrapping the coal wagons, which outnumbered the steam locomotives tenfold, thus requiring far more storage space. He could undertake the more difficult task of cutting up the steam locomotives, if and when the supply of coal wagons ran out. Consequently, the scene was set which would later make Dai Woodham a legend in the steam locomotive preservation movement.

Throughout the early 1960s, Dai Woodham's scrapyard at Barry became a graveyard for steam locomotives, with ever increasing numbers entering his yard until the end of steam in 1968.

Between 1959 and 1968, Dai Woodham purchased a total of 297 steam locomotives

from BR, out of which, eighty had been cut up for scrap during the nine-year period. The remaining 217 locomotives stabled in the sidings were largely intact as the firm was still engaged in cutting up the seemingly endless supply of coal wagons and other materials.

During the years that followed Woodham Brothers scrapyard became a household name amongst steam conservationists and preservation societies. It became a magnet for steam enthusiasts and people seeking to purchase spare and component parts from steam engines as well as buy the locomotives themselves. In 1979, the Barry Steam Locomotive Action Group was set up to negotiate the purchase of locomotives from Woodham Brothers on behalf of preservation groups and other potential customers.

Woodham Brothers scrapyard continued to trade for a further decade, whilst continuing to sell condemned locomotives for preservation. Barry scrapyard eventually closed in 1990 following the retirement of Dai Woodham. At the time of closure, there were just ten unsold locomotives left in the yard. They became known as the 'Barry Ten'. The local Vale of Glamorgan Council took possession of these locomotives, placed them into storage and over the next twenty years they were systematically sold for restoration and preservation or used for donor parts in other restoration and recreation projects.

Sadly, Dai Woodham died in September 1994 but he will be remembered for the important part which he played in the preservation of steam locomotives and the subsequent success of British heritage railways.

Of the 217 steam locomotives that were languishing in Barry scrapyard in 1968, a total of 213 were saved from the torch and rescued from the yard. 150 of these locomotives have already been restored and returned to steam and a further thirty-nine are in the process of being restored. Twelve have been dismantled and used to supply donor parts for other locomotives. The remainder are still in scrapyard condition at various locations and their future is yet to be decided.

The late Dai Woodham and his scrapyard are mentioned throughout this book, as the majority of locomotives referred to were rescued from Barry.

All the photographs in this book are of steam locomotives taken whilst they were operating on the railway network before being withdrawn from service and before they were preserved. Many of these locomotives can now be seen working on various heritage railways, whilst others are on public display in museums. A considerable number are frequently operating on the main line railway network, working special excursion trains and rail tours for steam enthusiasts and other members of the public.

LIST OF ABBREVIATIONS

BR = British Railways
BTC = British Transport Commission
C & WR = Canterbury & Whitstable Railway
ELR = East Lancashire Railway
G & WR = Gloucestershire Warwickshire Railway
GCR = Great Central Railway
GER = Great Eastern Railway
GNSR = Great North of Scotland Railway
GWR = Great Western Railway
IOW = Isle of Wight
KWVR = Keighley & Worth Valley Railway
LBSCR = London, Brighton & South Coast Railway
LCGB = Locomotive Club of Great Britain
L & MR = Liverpool & Manchester Railway
LMS = London Midland & Scottish Railway
LNER = London & North Eastern Railway
LNWR = London & North Western Railway
LSWR = London & South Western Railway
LT = London Transport
LYR (L & YR) = Lancashire & Yorkshire Railway
MR = Midland Railway
MOS = Ministry of Supply (War Department)
NBR = North British Railway
NLR = North London Railway
NRM = National Railway Museum
NYMR = North Yorkshire Moors Railway
RCTS = Railway Correspondence & Travel Society
SR = Southern Railway
SDR = Stockton and Darlington Railway
S&DR = Somerset & Dorset Railway*
SDJR = Somerset & Dorset Joint Railway*
SER = South Eastern Railway
SECR = South East & Chatham Railway
SVR = Severn Valley Railway
TVR = Taff Vale Railway
WD = War Department (British Government)

*S&DR and SDJR refer to the same railway company. The Somerset & Dorset Railway Company was formed in 1862 with the merger of the Somerset Central Railway and the Dorset Central Railway. The word joint was added to the company name in 1875 when it was agreed that the S&DR Company would be let jointly to the Midland Railway and the London & South Western Railway on a 999-year lease from 1876. Despite the name change, the word 'joint' was seldom used and the company, in the main, was still referred to as the Somerset & Dorset Railway.

Locomotive classification
UC = Unclassified; P = Passenger;
F= Freight; MT = Mixed Traffic

Types of tank locomotives
T = Tank Engine; PT = Pannier Tank Engine; ST = Saddle Tank Engine;
WT = Well Tank Engine

Classes of former Southern Railway Named Locomotives
V = Schools Class (all locomotives named after English public schools);
BB = Battle of Britain Class; LN = Lord Nelson Class; MN = Merchant Navy Class;
WC = West Country Class

Locomotives belonging to the above classes were given names associated with the Battle of Britain or the Royal Air Force (BB Class), Royal Navy Admirals (LN Class), Merchant Navy Shipping Lines, which used Southampton Docks, formerly owned and managed by the Southern Railway Company (MN Class) and West Country Resorts (WC Class).

CHAPTER 1

GWR – GREAT WESTERN RAILWAY LOCOMOTIVES

0-4-2T GWR 1400 Class Tank Locomotive, No. 1420

This 0-4-2 tank locomotive was built at Swindon in 1933 as a 4800 Class locomotive, number 4820. She was re-classified as a 1400 Class in 1946 and re-numbered 1420. She was assigned to Cardiff Cathays Shed in 1948, having previously worked from engine sheds at Pontrilas and Pontypool Road.

Number 1420 went on to work out of Fairford (Gloucestershire), Oxford and Exeter before spending her final years working on the Leominster to Kington

Former GWR 1400 Class tank locomotive, number 1420, pictured in steam at Hereford Shed in July 1964. (© PC)

branch out of Hereford Shed where this photograph was taken. 1420 was transferred to Gloucester Shed prior to being withdrawn from service in November 1964.

In 1965, 1420 was purchased by the South Devon Railway for preservation and has remained with and been owned by the railway ever since. She turned out to be a regular and very reliable performer over many years and is preserved in her original GWR livery.

0-4-2T GWR 1400 Class Tank Locomotive, No. 1442

This 0-4-2 tank locomotive was built at Swindon in 1935 as a 4800 Class locomotive, number 4842. She was re-classified as a 1400 Class in 1946 and re-numbered 1442. These 1400 Class locomotives were fitted with push-pull control apparatus for auto-train working

and were a familiar sight with their single auto-coach on many GWR branch lines. Number 1442 (shown) and number 1450 were the last remaining locomotives of this class when they were withdrawn from service whilst working out of Exmouth Junction Shed in May 1965. Both were subsequently preserved.

Number 1442 spent much of her working life in the Oxford and Buckinghamshire area. In her later years however, she could be seen working in the Tiverton area where she was nicknamed the *Tivvy Bumper*. After being withdrawn from service she was purchased by the late Lord Amory and put on display at Tiverton. In 1978, 1442 was moved into the Tiverton Museum of Mid Devon Life to afford protection against the weather. She is still on public display inside the museum, and a popular tourist attraction.

GWR 1400 Class tank locomotive, number 1442, pictured in GWR livery at an unknown location (possibly Slough), circa 1947. *(© PC)*

2-8-0 GWR 2800 Class Locomotive, No. 2807

This 2800 Class locomotive is the oldest privately owned preserved locomotive built by the GWR. This 2-8-0 locomotive, number 2807, was built at Swindon in October 1905 and worked out of Old Oak Common Shed in West London. In 1911, she moved to South Wales to work coal traffic. During the First World War she transported Welsh steam coal on a daily basis to Lancashire on the first leg of its journey to Scapa Flow to supply the Royal Navy Grand Fleet.

After the war, 2807 worked at various locations before being withdrawn from service at Severn Tunnel Junction in March 1963. She was later transported to Woodham Brothers scrapyard in Barry, where she languished for seventeen years, before being purchased by Cotswold Steam Preservation Ltd in 1981.

She was transported to Toddington on the Gloucestershire Warwickshire Railway where she was successfully restored and returned to steam in 2010. She has since remained with the Gloucestershire Warwickshire Railway and is fully operational.

2-8-0 GWR 2800 Class Locomotive, No. 2874

This 2-8-0 heavy freight locomotive, number 2874, was built at Swindon in November 1918. She started working out of Old Oak Common Shed in West London, hauling heavy coal trains from the South Wales Coalfield to London. Number 2874 was later moved from London and worked in a number of places in England and South Wales which were within the boundaries of the former Great Western Railway.

Number 2874 was withdrawn from service on 31 May 1963, just after the photograph shown here was taken. She was transported to Woodham Brothers scrapyard in Barry where she remained until 1987, when she was purchased for the Pontypool & Blaenavon Railway.

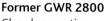

Former GWR 2800 Class locomotive, number 2807, pictured at Severn Tunnel Junction Shed on 3 June 1963, having been withdrawn from service. *(© MC)*

In the years that followed, 2874 went through changes of ownership until she was purchased by the 2874 Trust and based on the Gloucestershire Warwickshire Railway. She was subsequently transported to Toddington Works on the Gloucestershire Warwickshire Railway for restoration work to be carried out.

In September 2016 the boiler was removed and restoration work began. As of 2020, the slow painstaking work was ongoing, with funds still being raised to complete the project. No indication has been given as to how long the restoration work will take or when 2874 will return to steam. When she does enters service, she will join her sister locomotive number 2807 which is already preserved and working on the G & WR.

4-6-0 GWR 4073 Class Locomotive, No. 4079 *Pendennis Castle*

A total of 171 Great Western Railway Castle Class locomotives were built at Swindon between 1923 and 1950. Number 4079 *Pendennis Castle* was the seventh to be built in the first batch of ten, constructed between 1923 and 1924. She left Swindon Works on 4 March 1924.

In 1925, 4079 was loaned to the LNER to take part in locomotive exchange trials against the recently introduced LNER Class A1 Pacific locomotives, which were considered to be the most powerful passenger express locomotives in Britain at the time. The performance and fuel economy achieved by number 4079 outmatched the LNER Class A1s.

Former GWR 2800 Class locomotive, number 2874, pictured working an up empty coal train through Cardiff General Station in late May 1963, shortly before being withdrawn from service. (© MC)

Former GWR 4073 (Castle) Class locomotive, number 4079 *Pendennis Castle*, pictured in April 1925, departing King's Cross Station, London, with an express passenger train, consisting of LNER design coaches, during locomotive exchange trials between the GWR and the LNER. (© *MC*)

Upon completion of the trials, 4079 was exhibited at the British Empire Exhibition which was being held at Wembley Park from April to October of that year. She was exhibited alongside LNER Class A1 Pacific locomotive number 4472 *Flying Scotsman*, with a notice proclaiming *Pendennis Castle* as the most powerful passenger locomotive in Britain. Number 4079 continued working for the GWR and then BR until 1964.

Number 4079 was eventually withdrawn from service in May 1964 and purchased for preservation by a Mr Mike Higson.

In the years that followed, the locomotive saw several changes of ownership and spent over twenty-three years in Australia before finally returning to Britain in July 2000 following a ten week voyage. Number 4079 was in a state of neglect and in need of considerable restoration. Fortunately, 4079 is now owned by the Great Western Society at the Didcot Centre where she is undergoing a much needed overhaul before returning to service. It is anticipated that 4079 will be back in service sometime during 2020, when she will be able to give many more years of pleasure to members of the public by working charter trains, rail tours and special excursion trains on the main line railway network.

**Former GWR
4073** (Castle) Class
locomotive, number
4079 *Pendennis
Castle*, pictured at
Swindon Works on
19 August 1963. The
smokebox number
plate is missing from
the locomotive.
(© MC)

2-6-2T GWR 5101 Class (Large Prairie Tank) Locomotive, No. 4144

GWR 2-6-2, Large Prairie Tank locomotive, number 4144 was built at Swindon in 1946 and spent most of her life working as a banking engine in the Severn Tunnel, with the exception of a five year period between August 1957 and November 1962 when she was assigned to Tondu Shed (near Bridgend) engaged in working passenger trains in the valleys of South Wales. She was withdrawn from service in March 1965.

Number 4144 was sold for scrap but later purchased for preservation by the Great Western Society at Didcot in 1974. Restoration of the locomotive was completed in 1997 and 4144 remains working at the Didcot Centre with a boiler certificate valid until 2025.

**Former GWR Class
5101** tank locomotive,
number 4144,
pictured at Treherbert
(Rhondda) Station
on Easter Monday,
23 April 1962. She
is about to work a
Seaside Excursion
train to Blaenrhondda
and then through
the Rhondda Tunnel
into the Afan Valley,
before proceeding to
Aberavon (Seaside)
railway station on
the former Rhondda
and Swansea Bay
Railway. 1962 was
the final year for such
excursions, as railway
stations on the line
from Blaengwynfi
to Baglan Sands,
including Aberavon
(Seaside), closed that
December. *(© PC)*

2-6-2T GWR 5101 Class (Large Prairie Tank) Locomotive, No. 4160

GWR 2-6-2 Large Prairie Tank locomotive, number 4160 was built at Swindon in 1948 and assigned to Barry Shed in South Wales, to work local passenger services between the valley towns of Merthyr Tydfil and Treherbert (Rhondda) to Barry Island via Cardiff. During the mid 1950s she was transferred to Rhymney Shed, where she continued working local passenger services down the Rhymney Valley via Caerphilly and Cardiff, to Barry Island.

In May 1958, 4160 was assigned to Radyr Shed on the outskirts of Cardiff where she worked as a mixed traffic locomotive, before moving to Severn Tunnel Junction Shed in September 1964. She was withdrawn from service in June 1965, and sold for scrap. She languished in Barry scrapyard for almost a decade.

In 1974, 4160 was purchased by the Birmingham Railway Museum, and later the Plym Valley Railway. In 1990, she moved to the West Somerset Railway where restoration work was carried out, and in August 1993, 4160 formally entered service as a working locomotive on the West Somerset Railway at Minehead. She has remained a part of the West Somerset Railway ever since.

2-6-2T GWR 4500 Class (Small Prairie Tank) Locomotive, No. 4555

(Number 4555 has been given the name *Warrior* whilst in preservation.)

GWR Small Prairie Tank locomotive, number 4555 was built at Swindon in 1924 and allocated to Tyseley Shed in Birmingham. In 1948, the railways were nationalised and 4555 was assigned to Machynlleth Shed from where she worked in and around Machynlleth and Pwllheli.

In September 1957, 4555 was moved to South-West England, working from sheds at Westbury, Newton Abbot, St Blazey and Plymouth before being withdrawn from service in December 1963.

Former GWR 5101 Class, large prairie tank locomotive, number 4160, pictured working a goods train through Chalford, Gloucestershire, in August 1964. (© PC)

Former GWR 4500 Class locomotive, number 4555, pictured in front of a GWR 9000 Dukedog Class locomotive, at Machynlleth, Mid Wales, on 24 June 1956. *(© PC)*

After being withdrawn from service, 4555 was immediately purchased privately from BR for preservation. Despite being in good working order, she was given a light overhaul by BR at Swindon.

In 1973, 4555 started work on the Torbay Steam Railway which later became the Dartmouth Steam Railway and she has remained there ever since. Since working on the railway she has been given the name *Warrior*. Number 4555 is due to be hired out to the East Somerset Railway sometime during 2020 but will return to Dartmouth in 2023 to commemorate her fiftieth year with the railway.

4-6-0 GWR Hall Class (4900 Class) Locomotive, No. 4930 *Hagley Hall*

GWR 4-6-0 locomotive, number 4930 *Hagley Hall* was built at Swindon in 1929 and assigned to Stafford Road Shed in Wolverhampton. She worked on many parts of the GWR and Western Region of BR, working out of locomotive sheds as far afield as London, Birmingham, Bristol, Weymouth, Exeter and Swindon, before being withdrawn from service in December 1963.

After being sold for scrap, she remained in Woodham Brothers scrapyard at Barry, until she was bought by the Severn

Former GWR
4900 (Hall) Class
locomotive, number
4930 *Hagley Hall*,
pictured whilst
hauling a train of
empty wagons
eastbound through
Cardiff in August
1963. (© MC)

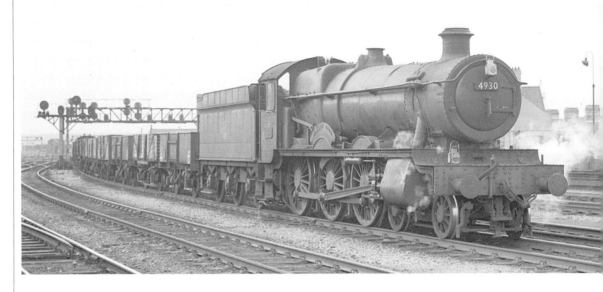

Valley Railway Holdings Company
in 1972. Restoration was carried out
at Bewdley and Bridgnorth and was
completed in 1979.

Number 4930 has since worked on the
Severn Valley Railway and has worked
numerous main line specials. She is
currently out of service for a much needed
overhaul but is expected to be back in
steam, working on the Severn Valley
Railway sometime in 2020.

4-6-0 GWR Hall Class (4900 Class) Locomotive, No. 4936 *Kinlet Hall*

GWR, 4-6-0 mixed traffic, 4900 Hall Class
locomotive, number 4936 *Kinlet Hall* was
built at Swindon in June 1929 and assigned
to Chester Shed. During her service with the
GWR and BR she worked at Shrewsbury,
Wolverhampton, Oxford, Banbury, Old Oak
Common (West London), Truro, Plymouth,
Newton Abbot and Cardiff before being
withdrawn from service in January 1964.

Former GWR
4900 (Hall) Class
locomotive, number
4936 *Kinlet Hall*,
pictured at Saltney
Junction near Chester
in July 1963. (© PC)

Number 4936 was later sold for scrap and transported to Woodham Brothers scrapyard in Barry where she remained until she was purchased for preservation by the Kinlet Hall Locomotive Company Ltd in 1980. After several moves, she was taken to Tyseley Locomotive Works in Birmingham for restoration and in February 2000, number 4936 successfully completed her steam trials some thirty-six years after being withdrawn from service.

She has since worked on the Llangollen Railway, East Lancashire Railway, Dartmouth Steam Railway and the West Somerset Railway, where she is currently based. Number 4936 has also worked main line excursion trains and is the oldest Hall Class locomotive running on the main line network. She is currently owned by J. J. P. Holdings (SW) Ltd.

4-6-0 GWR Hall Class (4900 Class) Locomotive, No. 4953 *Pitchford Hall*

GWR 4-6-0, mixed traffic locomotive, number 4953 *Pitchford Hall* was built at Swindon in August 1929 and assigned to Bristol Bath Road Shed. After nationalisation of the railways in 1948, 4953 worked out of Cardiff Canton Shed for over a decade, before moving to Swindon in 1959. She returned to Cardiff in 1962 after being assigned to Cardiff East Dock Shed, before being withdrawn from service in May 1963.

Number 4953 was sold for scrap and transported to Woodham Brothers scrapyard in Barry. She remained there until 1984, when she was purchased for preservation. She was restored at Tyseley locomotive works in Birmingham and made her first public appearance in over

Former GWR 4900 (Hall) Class locomotive, number 4953 *Pitchford Hall*, pictured at Cardiff East Dock Locomotive Shed on 13 April 1963 just a few weeks before being withdrawn from service. *(© MC)*

forty years at Crewe in September 2005, adorned in her original Great Western Railway livery.

Number 4953 later worked on several heritage railways and operated a number of main line charter trains. In 2011, 4953 was purchased by Mr Roger Wright, owner of the Epping and Ongar Heritage Railway which opened in 2012, and has continued to work there ever since.

4-6-0 GWR Hall Class (4900 Class) Locomotive, No. 4979 *Wootton Hall*

GWR 4-6-0 locomotive, number 4979 *Wootton Hall* was built at Swindon in February 1930 and assigned to Plymouth Laira Shed. During her service with the GWR and BR, she worked out of numerous engine sheds as a mixed traffic locomotive,

hauling a variety of freight and passenger trains all over the network. Number 4979 was working out of Oxford Shed when she was withdrawn from service in December 1963.

She was later sold for scrap and remained in Woodham Brothers scrapyard at Barry until 1986 when she was purchased by the Fleetwood Locomotive Centre. Little was done to the locomotive and she was sold on to the Furness Railway Trust in 1994, for use on the Ribble Steam Railway.

After years of storage, restoration finally started in earnest in 2016 and when completed, 4979 will be the largest locomotive working on the Ribble Steam Railway. It is not known how long the restoration will take.

Former GWR 4900 (Hall) Class locomotive, number 4979 *Wootton Hall*, pictured just north of the former Pontypool Road Railway Station, whilst hauling an empty coal train towards Hereford in July 1963. The locomotive is awaiting signal clearance and the driver can be seen alighting from the cab to contact the signalman on the lineside telephone. (© MC)

4-6-0 GWR Castle Class (4073 Class) Locomotive, No. 5029 *Nunney Castle*

GWR 4-6-0 locomotive number 5029 *Nunney Castle* was built at Swindon in May 1934 and assigned to Old Oak Common Shed in West London. She spent most of her working life hauling express passenger trains from London Paddington to the West Country and South Wales. She moved to Cardiff in 1962 and was withdrawn from service in December 1963.

After being sold for scrap, 5029 was transported to Woodham Brothers scrapyard in Barry. In 1976, she was purchased by the Great Western Society at Didcot and a consortium of private individuals. Number 5029 was later fully restored at Didcot and returned to steam in 1990, to work main line excursions and charter trains.

A further change of ownership took place in the 1990s and she was moved to Crewe by her new and current owner, Mr Jeremy Hosking. For the last twenty-five years, 5029 *Nunney Castle* has successfully operated on many parts of the national railway network. She has been well maintained, receiving overhauls in 2007 and 2017. Her 2017 overhaul has not yet been completed but she is expected back in service in 2020, when she will resume working main line rail tours and special excursion trains from her home base in Crewe.

4-6-0 GWR Castle Class (4073 Class) No. 5043 *Earl of Mount Edgcumbe*

GWR 4-6-0, locomotive number 5043 was built at Swindon in March 1936. Originally named *Barbury Castle*, she was re-named *Earl of Mount Edgcumbe* in 1937.

Number 5043 started life working out of Old Oak Common Shed in West London, hauling express passenger trains from London Paddington to the West

Former GWR 4073 (Castle) Class locomotive, number 5029 *Nunney Castle*, pictured at Cardiff General Station whilst working an up passenger train on Saturday, 1 June 1963. Two young boys standing on the station platform seem captivated by the locomotive. *(© MC)*

Former GWR 4073 (Castle) Class locomotive, number 5043 *Earl of Mount Edgcumbe*, pictured having arrived at Cardiff General Station with a down parcels train in August 1963. *(© MC)*

Country and South Wales. In 1952 she was transferred to Carmarthen Shed where she worked for four years before returning to Old Oak Common in 1956. In 1962 she moved to Cardiff before being withdrawn from service in December 1963 and sold for scrap.

Number 5043 was purchased from the Woodham Brothers scrapyard at Barry by the Birmingham Railway Museum in 1973. Initially, she was to be used as a spare parts donor, with the boiler destined as a spare boiler for number 7029 *Clun Castle*. However, it was later decided to restore her in her own right. The restoration was carried out at the Tyseley Locomotive Works in Birmingham and was completed in 2008.

After undergoing restoration at Tyseley, 5043 returned to steam in October 2008, painted in her 1950s livery, complete with BR double chimney. It was her first public appearance for almost forty-five years. Number 5043 has since worked numerous main line excursions and rail tours from her home base in Birmingham. In 2010 she worked a re-enactment of the GWR *Bristolian* express passenger train non-stop from Paddington to Bristol Temple Meads, including the return journey, to celebrate 175 years of the GWR. For this journey, she received the Rail-Tour of the Year award and just six months later she received the Performance of the Year award. It is hoped that 5043 *Earl of Mount Edgcumbe* will continue to build on her success.

Another photograph of former GWR 4073 (Castle) Class locomotive, number 5043 *Earl of Mount Edgcumbe*. In this photograph, she is pictured as a light engine at Cardiff General Station in August 1963. *(© MC)*

4-6-0 GWR Castle Class (4073 Class) Locomotive, No. 5051 *Earl Bathurst*

GWR 4-6-0 locomotive, number 5051 was built at Swindon in May 1936 and given the name *Drysllwyn Castle*. In August 1937, she was renamed *Earl Bathurst* and her original name was later re-allocated to locomotive number 7018. Number 5051 spent almost the whole of her working life assigned to Landore Shed in Swansea, working passenger trains to London and the Midlands. In 1961, she moved briefly to Neath Shed and then to Llanelli, before being withdrawn from service in May 1963.

She was sold to Woodham Brothers scrapyard in Barry, where she remained until she was purchased for preservation in 1970. Restoration took place at the Didcot Railway Centre and she returned to steam in 1979 in her former GWR livery and sporting her original name, *Drysllwyn Castle*.

Number 5051 has since worked numerous main line charter and excursion trains, displaying both the names *Earl Bathurst* and *Drysllwyn Castle* on different occasions. She is currently on public display at the Didcot Centre, awaiting an overhaul before she can return to main line service.

This spectacular **photograph** shows former GWR 4073 Castle Class locomotive, number 5051 *Earl Bathurst*, working hard as she starts an ascent up the northbound gradient after leaving Abergavenny Monmouth Road Station. She is working a Plymouth to Liverpool express passenger train on 28 October 1960. (© PC)

2-6-2T GWR 5101 Class Tank locomotive, No. 5193

(Converted during preservation to a GWR 2-6-0, 4300 Class tender locomotive number 9351.)

GWR 2-6-2, 5101 Class, tank locomotive number 5193 was built at Swindon in October 1934. She was assigned to Stourbridge Junction Shed and worked local passenger services between Wolverhampton and Birmingham Snow Hill for almost two decades. In October 1952, 5193 was moved to Truro and worked in Cornwall until she was transferred to Whitland, south-west Wales in 1960, then finally to Severn Tunnel Junction where she was withdrawn from service in 1962 and sold for scrap.

In 1979, 5193 was purchased from Woodham Brothers scrapyard in Barry and stored at Southport. She later moved to the Ribble Steam Railway before being sold to the West Somerset Railway at Minehead in 1998.

In 2000, it was decided to convert 5193 from a 2-6-2 tank locomotive, into a GWR 2-6-0, Class 4300 tender locomotive, but with a smaller boiler. The locomotive rebuild was successfully carried out, and in September 2004 the rebuilt locomotive and tender entered service on the West Somerset Railway. She was painted in GWR livery and re-numbered GWR 9351. She has since remained working on the West Somerset Railway.

2-6-2T GWR 4575 Class (Small Prairie Tank) Locomotive, No. 5538

Locomotive 5538 was built at Swindon in 1928 and worked on the GWR and BR, until being withdrawn from service in 1961. She was sold for scrap to Woodham Brothers in Barry. Number 5538 was later donated to the local County Council by Mr Dai Woodham, owner of the scrapyard, to be preserved and displayed in the town of Barry, as a reminder of the importance his scrapyard had played in the preservation of steam locomotives.

After some cosmetic restoration, 5538 spent five years on public display in Barry before being moved to the nearby Vale of Glamorgan Railway. She was later sold to the Dean Forest Railway where it was established that her frames needed replacing. Frames from condemned locomotive number 5532 were fitted to 5538 which was then sold to the Llangollen Railway for the restoration to be completed. It was only later realised that by fitting the frames from 5532 onto 5538, the identity of 5538 had been changed to that of 5532, as it is the frames which determine the identity of a locomotive.

The restoration of 5532 is still ongoing but she is expected to steam on the Llangollen Railway in the near future. When she does return to service she will only carry her original frames, number plates and shed plate. The main body, the wheels and all other parts of the locomotive, will be from locomotive 5538 which the late Dai Woodham had donated to be put on public display on the seafront in the town of Barry.

Former GWR 5101 Class locomotive, number 5193, pictured working a Newton Abbot to Kingswear passenger train at Torquay in July 1957. (© PC)

Former GWR 4575 Class locomotive, number 5538, pictured on 17 May 1960 at Perranporth, whilst working a local passenger service to Newquay, on the former Truro and Newquay Railway, which closed in 1963. *(© PC)*

2-6-2T GWR Class 4575 (Small Prairie Tank) Locomotive, No. 5553

One hundred 4575 Class locomotives were built between 1927 and 1929. They were a development of the GWR 4500 Class but with slightly larger side tanks to increase water capacity. They were designed as mixed traffic locomotives, primarily for use on branch lines and became known as 'Small Prairie Tanks'.

Former GWR, 2-6-2T, 4575 Class locomotive, number 5553, pictured near Wadebridge in Cornwall, whilst working a local passenger train from Wadebridge to Bodmin in May 1961. *(© PC)*

Number 5553 was built at Swindon in 1928 and was assigned to Bristol Bath Road Shed where she spent the next thirty years, with the exception of a few weeks in the summer of 1948 when she worked at Yatton. In December 1958, 5553 moved to Machynlleth before being transferred to St Blazey in November 1960. She was withdrawn from service in 1961.

After being sold for scrap, 5553 remained at Woodham Brothers scrapyard in Barry for over twenty-eight years, before being rescued by Pete Waterman for preservation. She was the last steam engine to leave the scrapyard in January 1990. Number 5553 was restored to working order in 2002 and put to work on the West Somerset Heritage Railway. In 2005, she visited the East Somerset Railway where

she took part in their spring into steam gala before returning to the West Somerset Railway. In 2012, 5553 was taken out of service in need of an overhaul after her boiler certificate expired.

In 2015, the Waterman Heritage Trust moved to the Peak Heritage Railway at Rowsley in Derbyshire and 5553 was taken there to await her overhaul. After she receives the overhaul, she will be put to work on the Peak Heritage Railway. Number 5553 continues to be owned by the Pete Waterman Heritage Trust.

4-6-0 GWR Hall Class (4900 Class) Locomotive, No. 5972 *Olton Hall*

Number 5972 was built at Swindon in 1937 and was assigned to Carmarthen Shed. She later worked out of numerous sheds in Wales and the West Country before being

Another photograph of former GWR 4575 Class locomotive, number 5553, pictured working a Bodmin to Wadebridge passenger train near Wadebridge in May 1961. *(© PC)*

Former GWR, 4-6-0, 4900 (Hall) Class locomotive, number 5972 *Olton Hall*, pictured hauling a southbound goods train at Abergavenny on 28 October 1960. (© PC)

withdrawn from service in December 1963 and sold for scrap. In 1981, she was purchased from Woodham Brothers scrapyard in Barry by a private buyer and restored at Wakefield in West Yorkshire. In May 1998, *Olton Hall* returned to steam for the first time in almost thirty-five years.

In 2001, 5972 *Olton Hall* received some prominence and much publicity after she was chosen to haul the *Hogwarts Express* in a number of Harry Potter films. Although she was painted crimson red (a fictitious railway livery) for the films and renamed *Hogwarts Castle*, she retained her original GWR number 5972.

In 2015 she went on public display at the Harry Potter Museum in the Warner Brothers Film Studios at Leavesden, near Watford, and will remain there for the foreseeable future. Her owner is Mr David Smith.

4-6-0 GWR King Class (6000 Class) Locomotive, No. 6000 *King George V*

Shortly after being built in 1927, *King George V* visited America to showcase British engineering. Her visit was a complete success and she was presented with a brass bell and plaque by the Baltimore and Ohio Railroad Company, which she continued to display after her return to Britain.

Number 6000 was considered to be a flagship locomotive for the Great Western Railway, working express passenger trains to and from Paddington before being withdrawn from service in 1962.

She was preserved as part of the National Collection and was restored at the Bulmer's Railway Centre in Hereford, which existed at the time. In 1971, 6000 was the first preserved steam locomotive in Britain to work on the main line,

which resulted in a steam ban which had been imposed in 1969 being lifted.

Number 6000 *King George V* was subsequently displayed for several years at the Swindon Railway Museum, before moving to the National Railway Museum in York in 2008. She is currently on public display in her original GWR condition at the National Railway Museum in York.

0-6-2T GWR 5600 Class Locomotive, No. 6697

GWR, 0-6-2 tank locomotive, number 6697 was a mixed traffic locomotive (5MT) built by Armstrong Whitworth of Newcastle in October 1928. A total of 200 of these locomotives were built, primarily to work in Wales, although they could be seen as far away as Wolverhampton, Swindon

and Bristol. They were sometimes given the nickname *Taffy Tanks*. They were ideally suited for working both heavy coal trains and passenger trains on the tight curves and steep inclines of the South Wales Valleys.

Number 6697 was the last steam locomotive to work at the Croes Newydd Shed in Wrexham and after she was withdrawn from service in May 1966, she was purchased directly from BR by the GWR Didcot Railway Centre for preservation.

She was transported to Didcot and could regularly be seen in steam until a flue tube collapsed whilst she was running in the late 1970s. She has since been on public display at the Didcot Centre pending repairs.

Former GWR, 4-6-0, 6000 (King) Class locomotive, number 6000 *King George V*, pictured outside Swindon works on 25 April 1954. (© PC)

Former GWR, Class 5600 tank locomotive, number 6697 pictured at Cardiff General Station, hauling a local passenger train from the Welsh Valleys to Barry Island in August 1959. *(© PC)*

4-6-0 GWR Modified Hall (6959 Class) Locomotive, No. 6989 *Wightwick Hall*

GWR 4-6-0 locomotive number 6989 *Wightwick Hall* was built at Swindon in March 1948 and was the penultimate locomotive requisitioned by the GWR before nationalisation took place on 1 January 1948. She left Swindon works on 31 March 1948, painted in GWR Brunswick Green livery with her number painted on the front buffer beam. She had the words BRITISH RAILWAYS painted on the tender in GWR style lettering. This contravened BR instructions that BR Black livery was to be used and green paint

Former GWR design (BR built), 6959 (Modified Hall) Class locomotive, number 6989 *Wightwick Hall*, pictured at Ebbw Junction Shed, Newport (South Wales), in August 1963. *(© MC)*

was not to be used after February 1948. Consequently, 6989 was repainted black in the early 1950s.

Number 6989 *Wightwick Hall* was assigned to Hereford Shed, where she worked successfully as a mixed traffic locomotive. Apart from a short period at Worcester between 1956 and 1957, 6989 continued working out of Hereford Shed until July 1959 when she returned to Worcester where she regularly worked the *Cambrian Coast Express* between Shrewsbury and Wolverhampton.

In September 1962, 6989 moved to Gloucester Horton Road, where she spent her last two years hauling fast freight before being withdrawn from service in June 1964. She was later sold for scrap and transported to Woodham Brothers scrapyard in Barry.

In 1978, 6989 was purchased by the Quainton Railway Society for preservation.

She was taken to the Buckinghamshire Railway Centre at Aylesbury in January 1978 for restoration work to be carried out. In June 2017 she was deemed fit to run. Painting was completed in October 2018 and she was returned to steam in December 2018. She is now fully operational and available for hire.

4-6-0 GWR Castle Class (4073 Class) Locomotive, No. 7029 *Clun Castle*

Number 7029 *Clun Castle* was built by BR at Swindon in 1950. She was assigned to Newton Abbot Shed to work express passenger trains between London Paddington and the West Country.

Apart from working at Plymouth in the spring of 1957, she remained at Newton Abbot until July 1962 when she was moved to Old Oak Common Shed and finally to Gloucester from1964 until her withdrawal from service.

Another photograph of former GWR design, 6959 (Modified Hall) Class locomotive, number 6989 *Wightwick Hall*, pictured working an up parcels train through Cardiff in 1963. (© MC)

Former GWR design, 4-6-0, 4073 Castle Class locomotive, number 7029 *Clun Castle* pictured hauling a two-coach local passenger service at Newton Abbot on 16 July 1957. (© PC)

Number 7029 was officially withdrawn from service on 31 December 1965 but she did work the following day. On Saturday, 1 January 1966, she hauled the 5 pm Gloucester to Cheltenham train, making her the last BR owned Castle Class locomotive to operate on the BR railway network.

In 1966, *Clun Castle* was purchased by Mr Patrick Whitehouse who later transferred ownership to '7029 Clun Castle Limited', who are the current owners. She was subsequently restored at the Tyseley Locomotive Works in Birmingham. Since then, she has operated tours all over the railway network from her home base in Birmingham and will continue to do so for the foreseeable future.

2-8-2T GWR 7200 Class Locomotive, No. 7229

Number 7229 was built by the GWR at Swindon in 1926 as a Class 5205, 2-8-0 tank locomotive, number 5264. In 1935, she was re-built with an extra pair of trailing wheels and re-classified as a Class 7200, 2-8-2 tank engine. She was re-numbered 7229. The Class 7200 were the first 2-8-2 tank locomotives to be built in Britain and the largest tank engines ever to work on the Great Western Railway.

Number 7229 worked for almost forty years on the GWR and later BR before eventually being withdrawn from service at Newport, Ebbw Junction Shed in July 1964. She was later sold for scrap.

In 1984, 7229 was purchased from Woodham Brothers scrapyard in Barry for preservation. She was transported to Bury on the East Lancashire Railway but it was not until 2015 that she entered the workshops for restoration work to be carried out. It is not known how long the restoration will take, or when it will be completed, but when 7229 does return to steam, she will be put to work on the East Lancashire Railway, who own the locomotive.

4-6-0 GWR Manor Class (7800 Class) Locomotive, No. 7819 *Hinton Manor*

Number 7819 was built at Swindon in February 1939 and assigned to Carmarthen Shed. She was transferred to Oswestry in 1943 where she spent the next two decades and could usually be seen hauling the '*Cambrian Coast Express*', a task which she regularly carried out. She was also occasionally seconded to perform duties at Whitchurch (Shropshire). She spent her final year working at Shrewsbury from where she was withdrawn from service in November 1965 and sold for scrap. She was later transported to Woodham Brothers in Barry.

In 1973, 7819 was purchased by the Hinton Manor Fund to be preserved for use on the Severn Valley Railway. In 1977, she returned to steam, fully restored in her former GWR livery. In the years that followed, 7819 successfully worked on the Severn Valley Railway and hauled main

Former GWR, **2-8-2T,** 7200 Class tank locomotive, number 7229, pictured hauling an up freight train through Cardiff in 1963. The smokebox number plate is missing from the locomotive. *(© MC)*

Former GWR, 4-6-0, 7800 (Manor) Class locomotive, number 7819, *Hinton Manor*, pictured working the up *Cambrian Coast Express* passenger train near Shrewsbury in April 1963. *(© PC)*

line services to destinations as far afield as North Wales and South Devon. She also spent time on loan to the Nene Valley Railway in 1994.

In 2004, ownership of 7819 was transferred to the SVR Charitable Trust and after further cosmetic restoration she was put on public display at the MacArthur Glen shopping centre in Swindon (site of the former GWR Works). Although she continues to remain on public display in Swindon, it is anticipated that she will be returning to the Severn Valley Railway in the near future.

4-6-0 GWR Design (BR built)
7800 Class Locomotive, No. 7820
Dinmore Manor

Number 7820 was built at Swindon in November 1950 and assigned to Oswestry

Shed where this early photograph was taken. During her time with British Railways she was assigned to no less than ten different locomotive sheds in Wales and the West Country before being withdrawn from service in 1965 and sold for scrap. Number 7820 then languished in Woodham Brothers scrapyard until, in 1979, she was bought by the Gwili Railway Company in Carmarthen who later sold her to Dinmore Manor Locomotive Ltd, her current owners. She was subsequently restored at Tyseley Locomotive Works in Birmingham and worked on the West Somerset Railway from 1995 until 2004 when she was taken out of service after her boiler certificate expired.

In 2014, 7820 was moved to a new base on the Gloucestershire Warwickshire

Railway where she worked until 2017. She spent the 2017 summer season working on the West Somerset Railway before returning to her home to the Gloucestershire Warwickshire Railway where she continues to work.

4-6-0 GWR Design (BR Built) Manor Class (7800 Class) Locomotive, No. 7828 *Odney Manor* (Renamed *Norton Manor*)

Number 7828 was built at Swindon in December 1950, and given the name *Odney Manor* although no such manor house exists. One possible explanation is that Lullebrook Manor (also named Odney Club) in Berkshire, adjacent to Odney Common, may have been referred to as Odney Manor in the past and the name used on 7828.

Throughout the 1950s, 7828 spent most of her time at Shrewsbury, often working the *Cambrian Coast Express* between Shrewsbury and Aberystwyth. In 1961, she moved to Wrexham and later Machynlleth, before returning to Shrewsbury, from where she was withdrawn from service in October 1965. Number 7828 was later sold for scrap and taken to Woodham Brothers scrapyard in Barry.

Number 7828 remained in Woodham Brothers scrapyard from May 1966, until June 1981 when she was bought privately for preservation and transported to the Gloucestershire Warwickshire Railway, where restoration work was carried out. It was completed in 1987. She later worked on the Gwili Railway, the Llangollen Railway, the East Lancashire Railway and the West Somerset Railway, who purchased her in 2004.

Former 4-6-0, GWR design (BR Built),7800 (Manor) Class locomotive, number 7820 *Dinmore Manor*, pictured as a light engine at Oswestry Shed on 22 July 1951. *(© PC)*

Former 4-6-0, GWR (BR Built), 7800 (Manor) Class locomotive, number 7828 *Odney Manor* pictured at Severn Bridge Junction, Shrewsbury, having just left the station with a southbound passenger train in April 1963. Severn Bridge railway junction is controlled from the signal box which appears in this photograph. It was originally a joint LNWR and GWR signal box, built in 1904. It is a three storey building of LNWR design and is the largest mechanically operated signal box in the world, with 180 levers. *(© PC)*

Another photograph of former GWR design 7800 (Manor) Class locomotive, number 7828 *Odney Manor*. In this photograph, she is in the railway sidings at Croes Newydd, Wrexham, in June 1962. *(© PC)*

In June 2011, *Odney Manor* was re-named *Norton Manor* after a Royal Marines Commando base which lies alongside the West Somerset Railway at Norton Fitzwarren near Taunton in Somerset. In 2016, 7828 was taken out of service for an overhaul. The boiler was serviced and re-fitted in August 2018 and 7828 returned to steam in December 2018 with a ten year boiler certificate. She is expected to continue working on the West Somerset Railway for many years.

0-6-0 GWR 9400 Class Pannier Tank Locomotive, No. 9466

These GWR designed pannier tank locomotives (classification 4F) were introduced in 1947 for heavy shunting and banking duties. Only the first ten were built by the GWR at Swindon between 1947 and 1948. A further 200 were built for BR by private contractors between 1950 and 1956. Number 9466 spent most of her life at Worcester where she worked from 1952 to 1961 on pilot and shunting duties, as well as working some local passenger and freight services.

She was built by Robert Stephenson & Hawthorn Ltd., Darlington, in 1952 and worked on the western region of BR until she was withdrawn from service in 1964 and sold for scrap. In 1977 she was purchased from Woodham Brothers scrapyard in Barry for preservation by Mr Dennis Howells. Restoration was completed in 1983, after which 9466 worked on several heritage railways. Sadly, Mr Howells the locomotive owner died in 2018, and 9466 was sold for use on the West Somerset Railway. However, the track system on the WSR will need to be upgraded before 9466 is allowed to use it. In the meantime, 9466 will operate on the Gloucestershire Warwickshire Railway until the end of 2020 when the matter will be reviewed.

Former GWR design (BR Built), 0-6-0, 9400 Class pannier tank locomotive, number 9466 (extreme left), pictured with other locomotives at Radyr sidings near Cardiff in August 1964, just days after being withdrawn from service on 31 July 1964. *(© MC)*

CHAPTER 2

SR – SOUTHERN RAILWAY LOCOMOTIVES

0-4-4T SR (LSWR) Class 02 Locomotive, No. W24 *Calbourne*

W24 was built in 1891 by the London & South Western Railway at Nine Elms and allocated the number 209. She started life on the mainland of England working at Fratton and Exeter. She passed into the ownership of the Southern Railway (SR number E209) when the railway amalgamations took place in 1923.

In 1925 she was transferred to the Isle of Wight, which was a part of the Southern Railway, and allocated the number W24. She was given the name *Calbourne*, which is the name of a village on the island. She was not displaying her nameplate when this photograph was taken, in 1965.

W24 continued to work on the Isle of Wight until being withdrawn from service in March 1967 when steam was dispensed with on the island.

Former SR (LSWR), 0-4-4, Class 02 tank locomotive, number W24 *Calbourne*, working a Ryde to Cowes passenger service on the Isle of Wight in August 1965. (*Photo © PC*)

A total of sixty Class 02 locomotives, designed by William Adams, were built at Nine Elms between 1889 and 1896. All sixty survived and went into SR stock in 1923 but withdrawals started in the 1930s. However, despite early withdrawals, forty-eight lasted into the 1950s and twenty-nine into the 1960s. The power classification given to these locomotives by BR was 1P.

When the above photograph was taken in 1965, locomotive number W24 did not have her nameplates fitted to the sides of the locomotive. Other photographs taken during the 1960s also show her running without nameplates.

The last two Class 02 locomotives to survive were W24 *Calbourne* and W31 *Chale*, which were both retained on the IOW after all the steam services were withdrawn. They were then used to haul the engineering trains which were being used to complete the Ryde to Shanklin electrification scheme which was taking place at the time. After electrification of the line was completed, both locomotives were withdrawn from service in March 1967. Attempts were then made to preserve both locomotives. W24 (*Calbourne*) was successfully preserved but unfortunately, the attempt to preserve W31 failed and she was scrapped in 1967.

W24 *Calbourne* was obtained directly from BR in 1967 by the Wight Locomotive Society, which became the Isle of Wight

Former SR (LSWR), 0-4-4, Class 02 tank locomotive, number W24 *Calbourne*, working a Cowes to Ryde passenger service on the Isle of Wight in August 1965. *(© PC)*

Another photograph of former SR (LSWR), 0-4-4, Class 02 tank locomotive, number W24 *Calbourne*. In this photograph she is pictured at Ryde locomotive shed on the Isle of Wight in August 1965. She is not displaying her nameplate. *(© PC)*

Steam Railway in 1971. She has since operated as the flagship locomotive on the Isle of Wight Steam Railway. The steam railway currently consists of some five miles of track which stretches from Wootton to Smallbrook Junction where it connects with the eight mile long BR electrified line from Ryde to Shanklin. The combined thirteen miles of railway is all that remains on the island, which once embraced almost sixty miles of picturesque railway.

In 2015, the National Railway Museum presented the IOW Steam Railway with a gift. It was an original nameplate from the LSWR Class 02 locomotive, number W24 *Calbourne*, which had apparently been removed from the locomotive whilst she was in service with BR and sent to the York Railway Museum. W24 is now fully operational and working on the Isle of Wight Steam Railway, proudly displaying her *Calbourne* nameplates.

The IOW Steam Railway has an envied collection of locomotives, consisting of some twelve steam locomotives and three diesel locomotives. Out of all these locomotives, W24 *Calbourne* is considered to be their flagship. W24 is the only surviving Class 02 locomotive in the world.

0-6-0T SR Class USA Locomotive, No. 30064

Number 30064 was built for the United States Army Transportation Corps in 1942 and shipped to Britain for the war effort. She was allocated WD number 1959. Whilst many of her class were shipped overseas, some, including 30064, were surplus to requirements and remained in Britain.

In 1947, WD 1959 was purchased by the Southern Railway and after some modifications she was put to work as a shunting engine at Southampton Docks. She was numbered SR 64 and re-classified as a USA Class 3F.

In 1963, 30064 moved to Eastleigh as a works shunter and from August 1966, she worked at Meldon Quarry on Dartmoor. She returned to Eastleigh in October 1966 and was withdrawn from service in July 1967.

Number 30064 was immediately purchased for preservation by the Bluebell Railway and placed into storage until 1971. She then worked on the Bluebell Railway until 1984 when she had to be withdrawn from service in need of an overhaul and extensive repairs. She has since been on public display at Horsted Keynes and it is anticipated she will remain there until funding is available for her overhaul to be carried out.

This final photograph shows former SR (LSWR) Class O2 tank locomotive, number W24 *Calbourne*, winding her way through the beautiful Isle of Wight countryside, hauling a five coach passenger train from Ryde to Cowes in the summer of 1965. *(© PC)*

Former SR USA Class, 0-6-0 tank locomotive, number 30064, pictured as a light engine engaged in shunting duties at Southampton in August 1965. *(© PC)*

0-4-4 SR (LSWR) Class T9 Locomotive, No. 30120

Number 30120 was built at Nine Elms in August 1899 and originally allocated the LSWR number 120. A total of sixty-six Class T9 locomotives were designed and built for express passenger work. They were given the nickname 'Greyhounds' in their early years, due to their fast acceleration whilst working at the turn of the nineteenth/twentieth century.

In 1923, locomotive number 120 was absorbed into the Southern Railway when the amalgamations took place and

Former SR (LSWR), 4-4-0, Class T9 locomotive, number 30120, pictured at Wadebridge Station, preparing to work a passenger train to Padstow in May 1961. *(© PC)*

she was re-numbered 30120 after the railways were nationalised in 1948. She continued working for British Railways and on 5 March 1960, she hauled the last passenger train on the former Didcot, Newbury & Southampton Railway between Newbury and Eastleigh, when the line closed to passenger traffic south of Newbury. Number 30120 was officially withdrawn from service on 31 July 1963, but continued to haul special trains until October 1963 when she was formally preserved as part of the National Collection.

After being withdrawn from service in 1963, 30120 became a part of the National Collection owned by the National Railway Museum in York and spent several years in storage at Fratton, Stratford and Brighton.

During the 1970s, 30120 was moved to the Birmingham Railway Museum at Tyseley before being taken to the National Railway Museum in York. In 1981, she was loaned to the Urie S15 Preservation Group who moved her to the Mid Hants Railway (Watercress line) where she worked for ten years. In 1991, 30120 was taken to the Swanage Railway, followed by the Bluebell Railway in 1993. She remained on sheltered public display at the Bluebell Railway until 2008, when she was transported to the Bodmin and Wenford Railway which became her temporary home base after she was given a full overhaul.

In 2017, number 30120 moved to the Swanage Railway and the NRM signed a loan agreement for her to remain there, until the end of September 2020 when she is scheduled for her next overhaul.

Former SR (LSWR) Class T9 locomotive, number 30120, pictured at Wadebridge Shed in Cornwall in May 1961. *(© PC)*

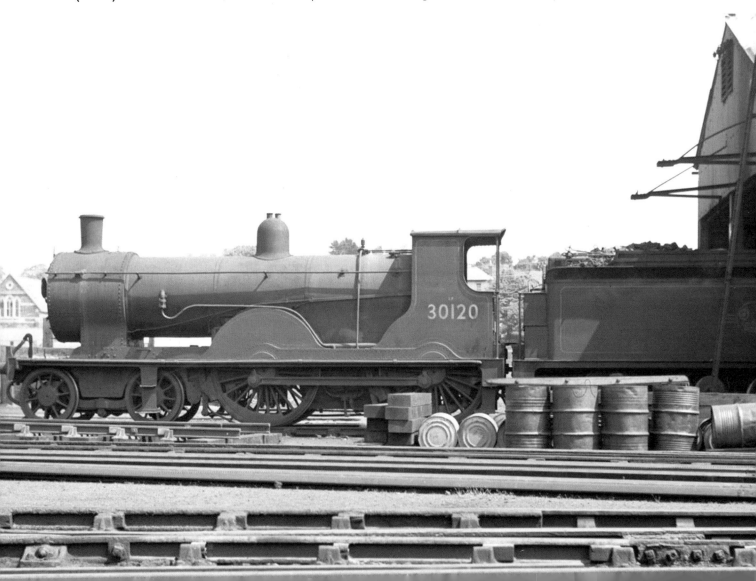

0-6-0 SR Class Q Locomotive, No. 30541

A total of twenty Q Class locomotives were built as basic goods engines (4F) just before the Second World War, and at the time the design was relatively old fashioned. Number 30541 is the only member of the class to have been preserved. The Q Class locomotives should not be considered to be on a par with the Q1 Class engines, which were much more powerful, efficient and versatile locomotives.

After being built, she was numbered SR 541 and assigned to Guildford Shed. In 1948, she was given BR number 30541 and worked out of Three Bridges (Crawley), Stewarts Lane (Battersea), Bournemouth, Basingstoke and Guildford locomotive sheds before being withdrawn from service in November 1964.

She was transported to Woodham Brothers scrapyard in Barry where she remained until she was purchased for preservation in 1973. Restoration was later carried out on the Bluebell Railway and she was returned to steam in 1983. She was painted in her original Southern Railway livery and carried her original SR number 541. In 2015 she received an overhaul and was turned out in BR Black livery, carrying her BR number 30541. She remains in service on the Bluebell Railway and is owned by the Maunsell Locomotive Society.

4-4-2T SR (LSWR) Class 0415 Radial Tank Locomotive, No. 30583

Number 30583 was built by Neilson & Co. Glasgow in 1885 and given LSWR number 488 (later 0488). She worked on the LSWR as a suburban passenger locomotive (power classification 1P). The term Radial locomotive refers to a locomotive (usually a tank locomotive) which is fitted with a leading, or more commonly a trailing, radial axle to reduce wear to rails and wheel flanges when working on curves. The device was also used on some nineteenth century carriages.

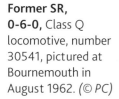

Former SR, **0-6-0,** Class Q locomotive, number 30541, pictured at Bournemouth in August 1962. *(© PC)*

Number 30583 was sold to the WD during the First World War. In 1923 she was purchased by the East Kent Light Railway to haul coal wagons. She was completely unsuitable for the task, so she was resold to the Southern Railway in 1946 to work passenger trains on the Lyme Regis branch line. She was ideally suited for this type of work and continued to work the line as BR 30583 until July 1961 when she was withdrawn from service.

She was subsequently purchased from BR for preservation by the Bluebell Railway and arrived there under her own steam. She continued working there until 1990, when she was put on public display, in need of a complete overhaul.

Number 30583 remains on display at Sheffield Park in East Sussex, awaiting her overhaul. She is the only surviving class 0415 locomotive in preservation.

2-4-0T SR (LSWR) Class 0298 Well Tank Locomotive, No. 30585

Number 30585 was built by Beyer, Peacock Ltd for the LSWR in 1874 and numbered 314 (later 0314). A total of eighty-five 0298 Class locomotives were built between 1863 and 1875. Designed by Joseph Beattie, these engines were referred to as Beattie Tanks and used primarily for working London suburban passenger trains. Eighty-two of the engines had been withdrawn from service by 1898, when the remaining three

Former SR (LSWR), Class 0415, 4-4-2, radial tank locomotive, number 30583, pictured at Lyme Regis, West Dorset, on 21 May 1960. *(© PC)*

Former SR (LSWR), 2-4-0T, Class 0298, well tank locomotive, number 30585, pictured at Wadebridge Shed in May 1961. (© PC)

(including 30585) were assigned to Wadebridge Shed in Cornwall, to work china clay trains on the Wenford Bridge mineral line. They continued working there for some sixty-four years before being withdrawn from service in 1962. They were given their new numbers after nationalisation in 1948.

Two of these locomotives were preserved. Number 30585 (shown) was purchased by the Quainton Railway Society (Buckinghamshire Railway Centre) and number 30587 was preserved as part of the National Collection, owned by the NRM in York. She is on long term loan to the Bodmin & Wenford Railway.

Number 30585 was restored and returned to steam in 1970. She has since worked on a number of heritage railways but remains based at the Buckinghamshire Railway Centre in Aylesbury. In September 2016 however, her boiler certificate expired and she was taken out of service for an overhaul. It is not known how long the overhaul will take, or when she will return to service.

4-6-0 LSWR Design (SR Built) Class S15 Locomotive, No. 30830

Locomotive 30830 was built at Eastleigh Works in August 1927 as SR number 830. A total of forty-five S15 locomotives were built between 1920 and 1936. They were a development of the Class N15 (King Arthur Class) and proved to be excellent for hauling mineral and heavy freight

trains, as well as working express goods trains. Predominantly built for freight duties, they were often used as mixed traffic locomotives. Locomotive 30830 was given her final number in 1948 and worked at Salisbury from then until 1963, before moving to Feltham. She was withdrawn from service in July 1964 and sold for scrap.

She spent over twenty years in Woodham Brothers scrapyard in Barry until she was purchased for preservation by the Bluebell Railway in September 1987. She was later sold to the Essex Locomotive Society, who relocated her on the North Yorkshire Moors Railway in 2000, for restoration.

In 2017, she was taken away from the NYM railway for restoration work to commence but no indication has been given regarding the current progress of the restoration, or when it is likely to be finished.

4-6-0 SR Lord Nelson Class (LN Class) Locomotive, No. 30850 *Lord Nelson*

Number 30850 *Lord Nelson* was built at Eastleigh in August 1926 and allocated SR number 850 (later, BR number 30850). Smoke deflectors were fitted in 1929. She was built as an express passenger locomotive (6P), to haul continental boat trains from London Victoria to Dover but was later used to work express passenger trains between London and the south-west of England. During her service with the SR and BR, *Lord Nelson* worked

Former SR 4-6-0, Class S15 locomotive, number 30830, pictured at Templecombe Station on 19 August 1963 working an up ballast train. *(© MC)*

Former SR, 4-6-0, Class LN locomotive, number 30850 *Lord Nelson*, pictured at Bournemouth Central on 19 June 1954. (© *PC*)

out of locomotive sheds at Stewarts Lane, Exmouth Junction, Nine Elms, Bournemouth and finally, Eastleigh from where she was withdrawn from service in August 1962.

After being withdrawn from service, *Lord Nelson* was preserved as a part of the National Collection. In 1979, she went to Carnforth where she was restored in her original Southern Railway Livery. She was later used to haul special excursion trains on the main line.

In 2009, *Lord Nelson* started work on the Mid Hants Heritage Railway (Watercress Line) after a long term loan agreement with the NRM. She will remain there for the foreseeable future and is the only surviving Lord Nelson Class locomotive in the world.

4-4-0 SR Class V (Schools Class) Locomotive, No. 30925 *Cheltenham*

Number 30925 was built at Eastleigh in 1934 as SR number 925 *Cheltenham* and assigned to Fratton Shed in Portsmouth to work passenger trains between Portsmouth and London Waterloo. After electrification of the line in 1937, she moved to Bournemouth and continued working trains to Waterloo. She later worked out of Dover Marine, Bricklayers Arms and Stewarts Lane, before moving to Basingstoke in August 1961, having been given her final number after nationalisation in 1948. Whilst there, 30925 worked numerous RCTS rail tours before being withdrawn from service in 1962.

After being withdrawn from service, 30925 became a part of the National

Former SR, 4-4-0 Class V (Schools Class) locomotive, number 30925 *Cheltenham*, pictured at York Station, double heading an RCTS Darlington to Nottingham (return leg) rail tour, together with LMS, 4-4-0, Class 2P locomotive number 40646 on 13 May 1962. Unfortunately, locomotive number 40646 was not preserved and was scrapped in September 1962. *(© PC)*

Collection owned by the NRM in York. Initially, she was put into storage but later visited several locations before returning to York for the 2012 Rail Festival. After the festival had taken place, the National Railway Museum signed a long term loan agreement for 30925 to be based on the Mid Hants Railway (Watercress Line). She has since continued to work on the Mid Hants Railway, proudly displaying her original Southern Railway number 925 and adorned in Southern Railway malachite green livery. Her boiler certificate is valid until 2022.

0-6-0 SR (SER) Class 01 Locomotive, No. 31065

Locomotive 31065 was built at Ashford Works as number 65 for the SER in 1896.

A total of 122 Class 0 locomotives were built between 1878 and 1899. Some were later rebuilt as Class 01 engines (including 31065). They were designed as freight locomotives (1F) but were later used for mixed traffic work on Kent branch lines.

After being withdrawn from service in 1961, 31065 was put into storage. She was subsequently purchased for preservation by Mr Lewis-Evans who transported her to Sheffield Park on the Bluebell Railway for restoration. Since being restored, 31065 has continued to work on the Bluebell Railway. She is the only surviving locomotive which was built by the former South Eastern Railway Company (SER).

Former SR (SER), 0-6-0, Class 01 locomotive number 31065, pictured at Hawkhurst in Kent on 11 June 1961, whilst working a Locomotive Club of Great Britain (South Eastern) rail tour, to mark the closure of the Paddock Wood to Hawkhurst railway line in Kent. Number 31065, together with former SR, 0-6-0, Class C locomotive number, 31592, worked the special train (double header), from Paddock Wood to Hawkhurst and back, before continuing to Tonbridge. Number 31063 was withdrawn from service just three weeks later. Both locomotives were subsequently preserved. (© PC)

0-6-0T SR (LBSCR) Class A1X Tank Locomotive, No. 32646

(Also worked on the Isle of Wight as Locomotive No. W8 *Freshwater*.)
Number 32646 was built at Brighton in December 1876 as LBSCR Class A tank locomotive number 46 (later 646) and given the name *Newington*. In 1903, she was sold to the London & South Western Railway as LSWR number 734 (no name), to work local passenger trains on the branch line from Axminster to the seaside resort of Lyme Regis.

In 1913, she was hired to the Freshwater, Yarmouth & Newport Railway on the Isle of Wight where she worked as engine number 2. After the 1923 railway amalgamations, she was absorbed into the Southern Railway Company and named *Freshwater* after a village on the island. In April 1932, she was re-numbered W8,

retaining her name, *Freshwater*. She continued working on the Isle of Wight until nationalisation of the railways in 1948. In May 1949, she was transported back to the mainland. Her nameplates were removed and she was allocated BR number 32646 to work on the Havant to Hayling Island branch line.

A total of fifty Class A1 locomotives were built between 1872 and 1880 (later rebuilt as Class A1X). They were nicknamed 'Terriers' or 'Rooters'. Some, including 32646, were nicknamed 'Hayling Billy' due to working the Hayling Island branch line from Havant. Number 32646 worked the line from 1949 until she was

withdrawn from service in November 1963. She was sold for preservation to the Sadler Railcar Company and three years later she was re-sold to Brickwoods Brewery in Portsmouth and put on public display on Hayling Island outside the Hayling Billy Public House, which was named after her.

In 1979, Brickwoods Brewery was taken over by Whitbread Wessex Ltd, who donated the locomotive to the Isle of Wight Locomotive Society, for use on the IOW Steam Railway. She received a new boiler in 1998 and has since continued to work the Isle of Wight Steam Railway as number W8 *Freshwater*.

Former SR (LBSCR), 0-6-0T, Class A1X, Terrier tank locomotive, number 32646, pictured at Hayling Island, Hampshire, whilst working a passenger train to Havant on 13 May 1961. *(© PC)*

Another photograph of former SR (LBSCR), 0-6-0T, Class A1X tank locomotive, number 32646. This time she is pictured at Hayling Island Station after arriving with a passenger train from Havant on 13 May 1961. A queue of passengers are leaving the station, having alighted from the train. (© PC)

0-6-0T SR (LBSCR) Class A1X Tank Locomotive, No. 32655 *Stepney*

Locomotive 32655 was built at Brighton in December 1875 as an LBSCR, Class A1 locomotive, number 55 (later 655), *Stepney*. She was rebuilt in 1912 as a Class A1X.

From 1916 until 1919, 32655 was on loan to the War Department and worked at the Woolmer Instructional Military Railway (later re-named the Longmoor Military Railway) in Hampshire. She subsequently worked on the Lee-on-the-Solent Railway as SR number 2655, until the line closed to passengers in 1931. She was then transferred to work on the Hayling Island line until 1938, when she was leased to the Kent and

East Sussex Light Railway which came under government control, to be worked by the Royal Engineers (Railway Operating Division) during the Second World War. In 1945, she returned to the SR at Fratton before working on the Southern Region of BR and was given number 32655 after nationalisation in 1948. She was eventually withdrawn from service in 1960 and purchased for preservation by the Bluebell Railway.

Number 32655 was the first ever locomotive purchased for preservation by the Bluebell Heritage Railway and she hauled the first train to run on the Bluebell Railway in May 1960. She has remained there ever since.

0-6-0T SR (LBSCR) Class A1X Tank Locomotive, No. 32662 *Martello*

Number 32662 was built at Brighton in 1875 as an LBSCR, Class A1 locomotive, number 62, *Martello*. She was rebuilt in 1912 as a Class A1X. A total of fifty Class A1 locomotives were built at Brighton. They were originally used to work suburban passenger trains out of London Bridge and Victoria until being replaced by the more powerful Class D 0-4-2 passenger tank locomotives, commonly referred to as D tanks.

Number 32662 was withdrawn from service in 1963 and purchased by Sir William 'Billy' Butlin for display at his holiday camp in Ayr. She was transported to the Bressingham Steam Museum, Norfolk, in 1971, after a change of ownership. She has since visited several heritage railways but remains based at the Bressingham Steam Museum where she can be seen on public display and at times, in steam, on the museum demonstration track. She remains privately owned.

Former SR (LBSCR), 0-6-0T, Class A1X tank locomotive, number 32655 *Stepney*, pictured in steam at an unknown location in the early 1950s. (© PC)

Former SR (LBSCR), 0-6-0T, Class A1X tank locomotive, number 32662 *Martello*, pictured working an LCGB rail tour on the former Kent and East Sussex railway line from Robertsbridge, East Sussex, to Tenterden in Kent, on 11 June 1961. This special commemorative train was the last train to run on the line, which closed the following day. *(© PC)*

0-6-0 SR Class Q1 Locomotive, No. 33001

Number 33001 was built at Brighton Works in March 1942 as SR number C1 (BR 33001). A total of forty Class Q1 austerity locomotives were built in 1942, to be used for moving the vast amount of wartime freight being transported through Southern England destined for mainland Europe. Due to their controversial shape and design they

were given nicknames such as 'Ugly Ducklings', 'Coffee Pots' and 'Charlies'.

Locomotive 33001 spent most of her early life working out of Guildford Shed. In 1958 she moved to Tonbridge, where the photograph was taken, and she was assigned to Feltham Shed in 1961. She returned to Guildford in 1963 and was withdrawn from service in May 1964.

After being withdrawn from service, 33001 was preserved as a part of the

National Collection, owned by the National Railway Museum in York. Number 33001 was on long term loan to the Bluebell Railway from 1977 to 2004, before returning to York where she is now on public display.

4-6-2 SR West Country Class (WC Class) Locomotive, No. 34010 *Sidmouth*

Locomotive 34010 was built at Brighton in September 1945 as SR number 21 C 110 (BR 34010). She was assigned to Exeter Shed to work express passenger trains between the West Country and London Waterloo. She was withdrawn from service in March 1965 and taken to Woodham Brothers scrapyard. In 1982, 34010 was purchased by Mr Graeme

Walton-Binns and taken to the North Yorkshire Moors Railway for restoration.

The NYMR later realised that they did not have the resources to restore 34010, so she was donated to Southern Locomotives Limited who operated on the Swanage Railway at Herston in Dorset (also Sellindge in Kent), who agreed to fund her restoration.

She remained there until October 2015, when a proposal was made at a Company AGM that the long awaited project to restore the locomotive would commence. Shareholders overwhelmingly accepted the proposal and finally, in the spring of 2016, the restoration work got under way. Due to lack of funds however, restoration work has since been intermittent and is expected to take several years to complete.

Former SR, 0-6-0, Class Q1 Austerity locomotive, number 33001, pictured at Tonbridge Station in Kent, double heading a former SR, 4-4-0, Class D1 number 31487, on a local passenger service in August 1959. (© PC)

Former SR, 4-6-2, Class WC (Rebuilt) locomotive, number 34010 *Sidmouth,* pictured as a light engine at Weymouth in August 1962. *(© PC)*

4-6-2 SR West Country Class (WC Class) Locomotive, No. 34023 *Blackmore Vale*

Locomotive 34023 entered service in February 1946 as SR number 21 C 123 (later BR 34023). Initially, 34023 was assigned to Ramsgate Shed but later worked out of Nine Elms, Salisbury, Exmouth Junction and Eastleigh before returning to Nine Elms. She was withdrawn from service on 31 July 1967 and purchased directly from BR by the Bulleid Preservation Society.

She was stored on the Longmoor Military Railway in Hampshire until its closure in 1970 (officially ceased operation on 31 October 1969), before moving to the Bluebell Railway where

Former SR, 4-6-2, Class WC (un-rebuilt) locomotive, number 34023 *Blackmore Vale*, pictured hauling an eastbound passenger service at Newton Abbot in Devon in 1957. It was not uncommon at the time for BR (SR) Pacific locomotives to use the former GWR main line between Exeter and Plymouth. *(© PC)*

she returned to steam in 1976. Number 34023 has since been the Flagship Locomotive of the Bluebell Railway but has been in and out of service due to mechanical problems and other issues. When out of service, she is frequently on public display at Sheffield Park, and despite her previous glitches, continues to be a star attraction on the Bluebell Railway.

4-6-2 SR West Country Class (WC Class) Locomotive, No. 34027 *Taw Valley*

Number 34027 was built at Brighton in April 1946 and allocated SR number 21 C 127 (BR 34027). Initially, 34027 was assigned to Ramsgate Shed before moving to Exmouth Junction, where she worked in Devon and Cornwall, hauling trains such as the *Devon Belle* and the *Atlantic Coast Express*. After

being rebuilt in 1957, she was transferred to Bricklayers Arms in South London and later worked out of Ramsgate and Brighton, before moving to Salisbury, where she was withdrawn from service in August 1964.

After being withdrawn from service, 34027 was sold for scrap and transported to Woodham Brothers scrapyard in Barry. She was later purchased by Bert Hitchen and Brian Cook for preservation and transported to the Severn Valley Railway in August 1985. Restoration was completed just two years later. She has since remained working on the SVR, but has spent considerable time hauling special excursion and charter trains on the main line network. She is expected to remain on the Severn Valley Railway for the foreseeable future, whilst continuing to work main line specials.

Former SR, 4-6-2, WC Class (Rebuilt) locomotive, number 34027 *Taw Valley*, pictured at Tonbridge, Kent, working a passenger train to Dover on 31 August 1959. *(© PC)*

4-6-2 SR West Country Class (WC Class) Locomotive, No. 34028 *Eddystone*

Introduced in May 1945, WC and BB Class locomotives were identical in every respect, apart from the names which they carried. West Country Class locomotives were given names of resorts in the west of England and were usually confined to working in the south-west of England. Battle of Britain Class locomotives were given names associated with the 1940 Battle of Britain and the Royal Air Force of that period. They primarily worked in the south-east of England, the area which was most associated with the Battle of Britain.

Number 34028 was built at Brighton in April 1946 and allocated SR number 21 C 128 (BR 34028). She was assigned to Ramsgate Shed, working Kent coastal passenger services into London Victoria. In 1948 she moved to Exmouth Junction, working passenger services from Devon and Cornwall to Salisbury. After being rebuilt in 1958, 34028 was transferred to Bournemouth to work passenger trains between Weymouth and Waterloo and also from Bournemouth to Bath on the former Somerset and Dorset Railway line, which closed in 1966. In May 1964, 34028 had the unfortunate infamy of being the first rebuilt Bullied Light Pacific locomotive to be withdrawn from service and sold for scrap.

In a twist of fate however, after languishing in Woodham Brothers scrapyard for over twenty years, 34028 was saved from the torch when she was bought by the Southern Pacific Rescue Group for preservation by Southern Locomotives Limited at Sellindge in Kent. In 1999, with the heavy work accomplished, 34028 was transported to Herston on the Swanage Railway in Dorset for restoration to be completed. September 2003 saw 34028 finally return to steam on the Swanage Railway.

After being returned to steam, 34028 *Eddystone* left the Herston works

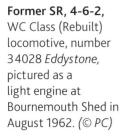

Former SR, 4-6-2, WC Class (Rebuilt) locomotive, number 34028 *Eddystone*, pictured as a light engine at Bournemouth Shed in August 1962. (© PC)

painted in her former BR Green livery. In the spring of 2004, she was put to work on the Swanage Railway where she has since remained. She has however visited a number of other heritage railways, including the North Yorkshire Moors Railway, the Bluebell Railway, the West Somerset Railway and the Churnet Valley Railway.

In 2014, 34028 was taken out of service for repairs and overhaul. She is expected to return to service on the Swanage Railway sometime during 2020.

4-6-2 SR Battle of Britain Class (BB Class) No. 34051 *Winston Churchill*

Number 34051 was built at Brighton in December 1946 as SR number 21 C 151

(BR 34051). She was originally un-named but was given the name *Winston Churchill* in September 1947. Number 34051 was initially assigned to Salisbury Shed to work express passenger trains between London Waterloo and Exeter. Apart from short spells at Nine Elms and Exmouth Junction Sheds, between January 1950 and May 1951 she spent her entire BR service at Salisbury until she was withdrawn from service on 31 October 1965.

Without doubt, the most important function performed by 34051 whilst in BR service occurred after the death of the statesman, Sir Winston Churchill, in 1965, when she was chosen to haul his funeral train.

On 30 January 1965, locomotive number 34051 *Winston Churchill* was centre-stage

Former SR, 4-6-2, WC Class (Rebuilt) locomotive, number 34028 *Eddystone*, working an up goods train at Upwey, Weymouth, in August 1962. (© *PC*)

Former SR, 4-6-2, BB Class locomotive, number 34051 *Winston Churchill*, pictured at Basingstoke, hauling a passenger train in the early 1960s. (© PC)

at his state funeral when she hauled a special funeral train from Waterloo Station in London to Handborough Station in Oxfordshire. This was the nearest railway station to Saint Martin's Parish Church in the village of Bladen, where Churchill's body was laid to rest.

After being withdrawn from service in October 1965, 34051 was preserved as a part of the National Collection, owned by the National Railway Museum in York. She was subsequently stored at Hellifield (North Yorkshire), Eastleigh and Preston Park (Brighton). After leaving Preston Park, she visited the Didcot Centre before arriving at the National Railway Museum in 1983 to be put on display.

Number 34051 was repainted in December 2014, to take part in an exhibition entitled 'Churchill's Last Journey', to commemorate the fiftieth anniversary of Churchill's death. The exhibition was held at the National Railway Museum in York, from 30 January until 3 May 2015. Number 34051 *Winston Churchill* was subsequently taken to the Locomotion Railway Museum at Shildon in County Durham and put on public display.

She can be seen on public display in the Locomotion Railway Museum at Shildon. She is the only preserved Battle of Britain Class locomotive never to have worked under her own steam since being withdrawn from BR service.

4-6-2 SR Battle of Britain Class (BB Class) No. 34059 *Sir Archibald Sinclair*

Locomotive 34059 was built at Brighton in April 1947 as SR number 21 C 159 (BR 34059) and assigned to Nine Elms Shed from where she worked passenger trains in and out of London Waterloo. She transferred to Exmouth Junction Shed in March 1951, followed by Salisbury Shed in 1955. Number 34059 was rebuilt in 1960 and continued working until she was withdrawn from service in May 1966 and sold for scrap.

In 1979, she was purchased from Woodham Brothers scrapyard in Barry, for preservation by the Bluebell Railway, without her original tender which had already been sold. A new tender was later built.

A long restoration process began in 1980 and a milestone was reached in 2009 when 34059 moved under her own steam for the first time in over forty years. Unfortunately, she has experienced more than her fair share of mechanical problems since then and she has undergone a series of expensive repairs. Despite the repairs which had been carried out, her mechanical problems persisted, and in August 2019 she was taken into the Bluebell Railway Workshops at Sheffield Park to be stripped down and given a full overhaul. It is not known how long the overhaul will take, or when she will be back in service.

Former SR, 4-6-2, BB Class locomotive, number 34051 *Winston Churchill*, pictured at Bournemouth on 4 April 1965, about to work an LCGB *Wessex Downsman* rail tour to London Waterloo. (© PC)

Former SR, 4-6-2, BB Class (Rebuilt) locomotive, number 34059 *Sir Archibald Sinclair*, pictured at Southampton, working an up express in August 1965. (© PC)

4-6-2 SR Battle of Britain Class (BB Class) Locomotive, No. 34067 *Tangmere*

A total of forty-four Battle of Britain Class and sixty-six West Country Class locomotives designed by Oliver Bulleid were built between 1945 and 1950. Number 34067 *Tangmere* was a Battle of Britain Class locomotive, named after an RAF Station near Chichester in West Sussex which was made famous during the Battle of Britain.

Number 34067 was built at Brighton in September 1947 as SR number 21 C 167 (BR number 34067). She was assigned to Ramsgate Shed where she worked until being transferred to Stewarts Lane Shed, south-west London, in November 1949. She remained there for over a decade. Number 34067 was one of a number of BB Class locomotives not to have been rebuilt during the 1950s/1960s, thus retaining her air-smoothed casing. In May 1961, 34067 was transferred to Salisbury and remained there until November 1963, when she

was withdrawn from service and sold to Woodham Brothers in Barry for scrap. She arrived there in 1965.

After being withdrawn from service, 34067 remained in Woodham Brothers scrapyard from 1965 until 1981 when she was purchased for preservation by a private buyer and transported to the Mid Hants Heritage Railway to be restored. Some restoration work was carried out on her in 1995, and in 1996 she was transported to the East Lancashire Railway for the restoration to be completed.

Locomotive 34067 returned to steam in 2003, after which she worked regular charter specials on the main line network until she was forced out of service in 2016 with serious firebox problems. She was put into storage on the West Coast Railways at Carnforth by her current owner, Mr David Smith. When she returns to main line service she is expected to operate from either the West Coast Railway base at Carnforth or the West Coast Railway base at Southall, West London.

Former SR, 4-6-2, BB Class locomotive, number 34067 *Tangmere,* pictured at Basingstoke in the early 1960s. *(© PC)*

Former SR, 4-6-2, BB Class locomotive, number 34067 *Tangmere,* pictured hauling an express passenger train through Tonbridge Station in 1959. *(© PC)*

4-6-2 SR (BR Built) Battle of Britain Class No. 34072 *257 Squadron*

This locomotive was built at Brighton in April 1948 and entered service on BR, Southern Region working out of Dover Marine Shed, having been allocated BR number 34072. Her main duties consisted of working passenger boat trains between London and Dover and local passenger services from the Kent coast to Charing Cross. In 1958, after the Kent coast lines were electrified, she was transferred to Exmouth Junction Shed. From there, she worked passenger services from Salisbury, to Devon and Cornwall. This was an unfamiliar area, not normally worked by BB Class locomotives, who traditionally worked in south-east England.

In June 1964, 34072 was transferred to Eastleigh Shed, before being withdrawn from service just four months later. She was sold for scrap and transported to Woodham Brothers scrapyard. At the time 34072 was withdrawn from service, she was less than seventeen years old, but unlike a number of her sister locomotives she had never been rebuilt, thus retaining her original air-smoothed casing. Number 34072 remained in Woodham Brothers scrapyard until November 1984, when she was purchased by Southern Locomotives Ltd (Swanage Heritage Railway) for preservation and taken to the Swindon & Cricklade Heritage Railway at Blunsdon in Wiltshire. She entered Swindon Works in 1987 where restoration work was carried out. Number 34072 was fully restored just in time for her to take part in the fiftieth anniversary celebration of the Battle of Britain, which was held at Folkestone in September 1990.

She continued working throughout the 1990s, visiting numerous heritage

Former SR design (BR Built), 4-6-2, BB Class locomotive, number 34072, *257 Squadron*, pictured at Wadebridge in May 1961, working a Waterloo to Padstow passenger train. (© PC)

railways until she had to be withdrawn from service in January 2003 as a result of serious fire-box problems. Repairs were subsequently carried out, followed by an overhaul. In September 2018, 34072 returned to service on the Swanage Railway in Dorset and is now fully operational. She continues to be owned by Southern Locomotives Limited.

4-6-2 SR (BR Built) West Country Class (WC Class) No. 34092 *City of Wells*

Number 34092 was built at Brighton in September 1949. Originally named *Wells*, she was re-named *City of Wells* just two months later. After entering service, 34092

was assigned to Stewarts Lane Shed in South London to work boat trains from London Victoria to Dover and Folkestone. This included the prestigious *Golden Arrow* express which was steam hauled until 1961, when the line was electrified. Number 34092 was then moved to Salisbury where she worked express passenger trains between Exeter and Waterloo until she was withdrawn from service in November 1964 and sold to Woodham Brothers scrapyard.

In 1971 she was purchased for preservation and restored in 1979 to work on the Keighley & Worth Valley Railway. She subsequently visited several heritage railways and worked main line

Former SR design BR Built), 4-6-2, BB Class locomotive, number 34072, *257 Squadron* pictured on a turntable at Bricklayers Arms Shed in South London circa 1955. (© *PC*)

Former SR design (BR Built), 4-6-2, WC Class locomotive, number 34092 *City of Wells*, pictured working the down *Golden Arrow* express through Tonbridge on 31 August 1959. *(© PC)*

excursion trains, carrying her two names, *Wells* and *City of Wells* on different occasions.

In 2015, 34092 was loaned to the East Lancashire Railway who then purchased her from the KWVR in March 2019. She is currently fully operational and can be seen working on the East Lancashire Railway.

4-6-2 SR (BR Built) West County Class (WC Class) No. 34101 *Hartland*

Number 34101 was built at Eastleigh in February 1950 and entered BR Southern Region service working out of Stewarts Lane Shed in South London, hauling express passenger and boat train services, including the *Golden Arrow*, from Victoria to Dover and Folkestone.

She was rebuilt in 1960 and continued working from Victoria until the line was electrified in 1961, when she was transferred to Bricklayers Arms. Locomotive 34101 was then moved three times in quick succession to Brighton, Nine Elms and Eastleigh from where she was withdrawn from service in July 1966. She was one of only six Bulleid design WC & BB Class light Pacific locomotives to have been built at the Eastleigh Works and the only one to survive into preservation.

After being withdrawn from service, 34101 was sold for scrap and transported to Woodham Brothers scrapyard.

Locomotive 34101 languished in Woodham Brothers scrapyard from

Former SR design (BR Built), 4-6-2, WC Class locomotive, number 34101 *Hartland,* pictured at Folkestone Warren, working the up *Golden Arrow* express on 5 May 1961. *(© PC)*

Former SR design (BR Built), 4-6-2, WC Class locomotive, number 34101 *Hartland,* pictured working the down *Golden Arrow* express through Folkestone Central on 6 June 1961. *(© PC)*

October 1966 until 1978, when she was purchased for preservation by Mr Richard Shaw (Shaw Metals Ltd, Derby) and transported to the North Yorkshire Moors Railway. Restoration work was carried out and she was successfully steam tested in 1993 and entered service on the NYMR in 1994.

Number 34101 has since worked on the NYMR but did spend some time on loan to the Great Central Railway at Loughborough before returning home to the NYMR. In 2014, 34101 was taken out of service again for a further overhaul, during which time her owner, Richard Shaw, sadly died. Ownership was passed to his wife and daughters who decided that 34101 should remain based on the North Yorkshire Moors Railway. Number 34101 *Hartland* continues to work the NYMR and will hopefully give many more years of service there.

Former SR, 4-6-2, Rebuilt MN Class locomotive, number 35005 *Canadian Pacific*, pictured at Templecombe Station on 19 August 1963 working an up express passenger train to London Waterloo. (© MC)

4-6-2 SR (Rebuilt) Merchant Navy Class (MN Class) No. 35005 *Canadian Pacific*

A total of thirty Merchant Navy Class locomotives were built between 1941 and 1949. They were all later rebuilt. Number 35005 was built at Eastleigh in December 1941 as SR number 21C5 (BR 35005), designed to haul the heavy boat train services from London Victoria to Dover and Folkestone. She initially entered service during the Second World War, when ferry services to Europe were suspended and boat train services were not operating, so 35005 was used instead to work express passenger services on the main lines from London Waterloo to Southampton and Exeter. She worked out of Exmouth Junction, Nine Elms, Bournemouth and Weymouth Sheds during her time in SR and BR service. She received her rebuild in 1959.

Locomotive 35005 was withdrawn from service in October 1965 but was later preserved. She subsequently hauled main line specials and went through changes of ownership until being purchased by the Mid Hants Railway Preservation Society in 2006. She has since remained based on the Mid Hants Railway where she works and is considered to be their flagship locomotive. Number 35005 is, however, currently undergoing a complete overhaul and is unlikely to be back in service before the summer of 2021.

4-6-2 SR (Rebuilt) Merchant Navy Class (MN Class) Locomotive, No. 35006 *Peninsular & Oriental Steam Navigation Company*

Number 35006 was built at Eastleigh in December 1941 and allocated SR number 21 C 6 (BR 35006). She was assigned to Salisbury Shed where she remained for her entire service. She was rebuilt in October 1959.

She was withdrawn from service in August 1964 and sold for scrap to Woodham Brothers. In 1983, 35006 was bought for preservation by the 35006 Locomotive Company and taken to Toddington on the Gloucestershire Warwickshire Steam Railway for restoration work to be carried out.

On 16 May 2016, after a long and meticulous overhaul including building a new tender, 35006 entered service once again. She immediately hauled her first passenger train in over fifty years, when she took a fourteen coach passenger train on two return trips to Cheltenham. In 2017, she took part in a summer gala on the Mid Hants Heritage Railway before returning to her home base, which is the Gloucestershire Warwickshire Railway. It is hoped that she will steam on for many years to come.

Former SR, 4-6-2, Rebuilt MN Class locomotive, number 35006 *Peninsular & Oriental Steam Navigation Company*, pictured working a down express at Templecombe in August 1963. *(© MC)*

4-6-2 SR (Rebuilt) Merchant Navy Class (MN Class) Locomotive, No. 35022 *Holland-America Line*

Locomotive 35022 was built for British Railways (Southern Region) at Eastleigh Works in 1948. She was assigned to Exmouth Junction Shed as an un-named locomotive to work express passenger services to London Waterloo. She was moved to Bournemouth in 1954 where she continued working main line passenger trains. After working for more a decade, she was finally given the name *Holland-America Line* at a naming ceremony which took place at Southampton Docks in 1959.

She returned to Exmouth Junction the following year and later worked at Nine Elms and Weymouth from where she was withdrawn from service in 1966. She was sold for scrap and remained at Woodham Brothers scrapyard until she was bought for preservation by the Southern Steam Trust in 1983.

Number 35022 subsequently went through change of ownership and spent many years in storage. Her future however, seems to be much brighter. She is currently owned by Mr Jeremy Hosking and has been taken to the LNWR Heritage Centre at Crewe for her long awaited restoration to be carried out.

Former SR design, (BR Built), 4-6-2, Rebuilt MN Class locomotive, number 35022, *Holland-America Line*, pictured working a down express passenger train at Southampton in August 1965. (© PC)

CHAPTER 3

LMS – LONDON, MIDLAND AND SCOTTISH RAILWAY LOCOMOTIVES

2-6-2T LMS (BR Built) Class 2 Tank locomotive, No. 41298

Locomotive 41298 was built at Crewe in October 1951 and assigned to Bricklayers Arms Shed in South London as a pilot engine, which involved shunting empty passenger stock in and out of Victoria Station.

In 1953, she moved to North Devon, working branch line services in the Barnstaple area for almost ten years before

transferring to Weymouth to work empty boat-train stock.

In October 1966, 41298 was assigned to Nine Elms Shed to work as a pilot engine at Waterloo Station before being withdrawn from service in July 1967. After being withdrawn from service, 41298 was purchased directly from BR by the Ivatt Locomotive Trust for preservation and was transported to

Former LMS (BR Built), 2-6-2T, Class 2 tank locomotive, number 41298, pictured at Waterloo Station whilst shunting empty stock on 18 June 1967. (© PC)

the Buckinghamshire Railway Centre at Quainton in 1970, where restoration work was carried out.

Number 41298 was subsequently moved to the Isle of Wight Steam Railway, where she hauled her first passenger train in 2015. She has since been in regular service on the Isle of Wight Steam Railway and she is expected to remain there for many years.

2-6-4T LMS (BR Built) Class 4MT Tank Locomotive, No. 42073

Number 42073 was built at Brighton in November 1950 and entered service on BR Southern Region at Stewarts Lane Shed in South London where she spent a mere three months before moving to work at Ashford and Dover.

In 1954, 42073 was transferred to Gateshead in the north-eastern Region of BR. The following year, on 19 April 1955,

42073 was in a collision with Class V2 locomotive number 60968, when both locomotives converged onto the same line on a diamond crossing at Newcastle. Both locomotives were derailed and suffered extensive damage.

Number 42073 was transferred to Hammerton Street Depot, Bradford, in 1957, followed by a number of moves within the County of Yorkshire in quick succession. She worked out of Sowerby Bridge, York, Leeds Neville Hill, Bradford Low Moor, Wakefield, Leeds Copley Hill, Ardsley and Normanton near Wakefield, from where she was withdrawn from service in October 1967.

After being withdrawn from service, 42073 was purchased from BR by the Lakeside Railway Estates Company and stored in Carnforth for preservation. In 1970, the Lakeside and Haverthwaite Railway Company was formed in 1973

Former LMS design (BR Built) 2-6-4T, Class 4MT tank locomotive, number 42073, pictured working a local Whitby to Malton passenger train at Malton, North Yorkshire, on 26 August 1958. (© PC)

Another photograph of former LMS Fairburn design, Class 4MT, tank locomotive, number 42073. In this picture, she has replaced a broken down diesel multiple unit to work a local passenger service from Pontefract Baghill Station to Leeds. Number 42073 is pictured using the Pontefract Baghill to Monkhill branch line, which closed in 1964. The photograph was taken on 3 April 1961. (© PC)

and number 42073 hauled the first train on the newly opened railway, along with her sister locomotive number 42085. Number 42073 is still fully operational on the Lakeside and Haverthwaite Heritage Railway in Cumbria.

A total of 277 of these 2-6-4T, Fairburn mixed traffic tank locomotives were built at Derby and Brighton Works between 1945 and 1951. Only two of the class have been preserved. This locomotive and a sister locomotive, number 42085, are both preserved on the Lakeside and Haverthwaite Heritage Railway.

2-6-4T LMS Class 4P Locomotive, No. 42500

Number 42500 was built at Derby in March 1934 as LMS number 2500 (BR 42500) and assigned to Shoeburyness Shed where she spent her entire working life. She was primarily designed to work passenger services from London, Fenchurch Street to Tilbury, Southend and Shoeburyness. Number 42500 was the first ever Stanier 2-6-4 tank engine to be built. She had three cylinders to give her rapid acceleration between the many frequent station stops that existed on the Fenchurch Street line.

Former LMS 2-6-4T, Class 4P tank locomotive, number 42500, pictured in steam at Shoeburyness in Essex in the early 1950s. *(© PC)*

Locomotive 42500 was withdrawn from service in June 1962 and preserved as a part of the National Collection. She is currently based at the National Railway Museum in York, where she is on public display in the main hall. She is painted in LMS lined black livery and carries her LMS number 2500. She is the only locomotive of her class (out of a total of thirty-seven) to have been preserved and is expected to remain on display at York Railway Museum for the foreseeable future.

2-6-0 LMS Class 5MT Crab Locomotive, No. 42700

Locomotive 42700 was built at Horwich Works, Bolton, in June 1926. She was the first of 245 such locomotives to be built. The first 100 locomotives of the class (including 42700) were initially painted in crimson lake colour livery and 42700 was allocated LMS number 13000. In 1933, she was renumbered and was allocated LMS number 2700. The BR number 42700 was given to her after nationalisation took place in 1948.

Number 42700 spent almost all of her working life operating in Lancashire and West Yorkshire until she was withdrawn from service in March 1966 after almost forty years service. She was preserved as part of the National Collection and initially placed into storage at Hellifield.

In 1968, 42700 was taken out of storage and transported to Keighley, on loan to the Keighley & Worth Valley Heritage Railway.

Former LMS 2-6-0, Class 5MT Crab locomotive, number 42700, pictured at Pontefract Monkhill Station, working a Knottingley to Wakefield local passenger service in October 1955. *(© PC)*

Former LMS 2-6-0, Class 5MT Crab locomotive, number 42700, pictured in steam, on standby duties in the railway sidings at York Shed in 1962. *(© PC)*

After some minor work was carried out, she returned to steam and became operational.

During the 1970s, 42700 was painted in black LMS livery, bearing her LMS number 2700, before being loaned to the East Lancashire Railway. She also spent time at the Barrow Hill Roundhouse near Chesterfield in Derbyshire before being taken to the National Railway Museum at Shildon in County Durham. Whilst there, she was again repainted and in 2010 she emerged from the paint shop in her original LMS crimson lake livery and bearing her original LMS number 13000. She remained on display at Shildon before returning home to the National Railway Museum in York.

She is now proudly on display at the National Railway Museum in York, adorned in her original LMS crimson lake livery and displaying her original LMS number 13000. She remains a part of the National Collection.

Former LMS 0-6-0, Class 4F locomotive, number 44422, pictured hauling a local passenger service on the former Somerset & Dorset Railway line at Templecombe in 1964. *(© PC)*

0-6-0 LMS Fowler Class 4F Locomotive, No. 44422

Locomotive 44422 was built at Derby in October 1927 as LMS number 4422 (BR 44422). These Fowler locomotives were primarily designed for freight duties but it was not unusual to see them hauling passenger trains as shown in the photograph. Number 44422 spent most of her working life in south-west England before being withdrawn from service in June 1965 and sold for scrap.

In 1977 she was purchased for preservation from Woodham Brothers scrapyard by the 44422 Locomotive Company for use on the Churnet Valley Railway (North Staffordshire Heritage Railway). After a long period of restoration, 44422 moved under her own steam in September 1990.

She subsequently worked on numerous heritage railways, including the Churnet Valley Railway, Llangollen Railway, East Lancashire Railway, Nene Valley

Railway, Great Central Railway and the North Norfolk Railway.

After a further overhaul in 2013, 44422 was transported to Bishops Lydeard to work on the West Somerset Railway at Minehead on a twenty-five year lease. In 2019 an unexpected announcement was made that the West Somerset Railway had terminated the twenty-five year lease contract, and a new home is currently being sought for the locomotive.

4-6-0 LMS Stanier Class 5 (Black 5) locomotive, No. 44767

(Number 44767 was allocated the name *George Stephenson* after being preserved.)

Locomotive 44767 was built at Crewe on 31 December 1947 and allocated LMS number 4767, quickly followed by BR number 44767. Out of a total of 842 Class 5 locomotives to be built,

44767 was unique in that she featured the Stephenson valve gear and sported a double chimney. The double chimney was removed in 1953.

She was withdrawn from BR service in December 1967 and sold to Mr Brian Hollingsworth who later re-sold her to Mr Ian Storey, Chairman of the North Eastern Locomotive Preservation Group. Restoration was later carried out and completed in 1975. She was then given the name *George Stephenson*. She had never previously carried a name.

Number 44767 then spent over forty years working on numerous heritage railways until, in September 2018, it was announced that West Coast Railways had purchased 44767 from Mr Ian Storey. Number 44767 was taken to her new home at Carnforth where she is currently awaiting an overhaul before returning to service.

Former LMS 4-6-0, Class 5 (Black Five) locomotive, number 44767, pictured as a light engine at Pontefract Tanshelf Railway Station on 1 May 1958. (© PC)

4-6-0 LMS Stanier Class 5 (Black 5) Locomotive, No. 44781

On 11 August 1968, 44781 received some prominence after being one of the four locomotives selected to work the famous 'Fifteen Guinea Special', the last BR steam-hauled passenger service. The others were Britannia Class locomotive, number 70013 *Oliver Cromwell* and two other black fives, 44871 and 45110.

After the event, 70013 *Oliver Cromwell* was preserved by BR as a part of the National Collection and the three Class 5 locomotives were bought privately from BR for immediate preservation.

Number 44871 was put on display at Steamtown Museum, Carnforth (now closed) until the main line steam ban was lifted in 1972. She then worked special excursions on the main line in the north east of England. During the 1980s and 1990s she worked passenger train services on the West Highland Line in Scotland. She regularly worked on the NYM Railway but is now working on the East Lancashire Railway where she is currently based.

Number 45110 was also preserved immediately after working the 'Fifteen Guinea Special' and eventually found a new home on the Severn Valley Railway. She is currently on public display at the Highley Engine House whilst awaiting an overhaul.

Number 44781 was bought by the Columbia Film Company, initially to be used in the film *The Virgin Soldiers*, before being resold to Mr Gerald Pagano, a Saffron Walden businessman, for long term preservation. Mr Pagano had previously purchased and preserved a Sentinel steam locomotive.

After the successful filming, a dispute took place between Mr Pagano and BR over the cost of recovering 44781 from the film site. The dispute culminated with a local scrap metal dealer visiting the site, cutting the locomotive up *in situ* before disposing of her, thus curtailing her prearranged long term preservation. Number 44781 had been preserved for less than five months, by far the shortest period of time that any locomotive in British history has spent in preservation. She could well be remembered as the 'ill-fated black five'.

Former LMS 4-6-0, Class 5 (Black 5) locomotive, number 44781, at York Station, working a York to Manchester passenger train in the summer of 1960. The two schoolboys inside the cab are myself (author) Malcolm Clegg and my younger brother Geoff, who is looking out of the cab window. The strap over my shoulder is attached to the case of a 1950s Kodak Brownie box camera, my first ever film camera, which led to my lifelong interest in photography. *(© PC)*

4-6-0 LMS Stanier Class 5 (Black 5) Locomotive, No. 45293

Locomotive 45293 was built in December 1937 by Armstrong Whitworth of Newcastle as LMS number 5293. She entered service at Shrewsbury where she worked mixed traffic trains to and from Swansea. Over the next five years she was moved several times before being assigned to Carlisle Upperby Shed where she spent the next twenty years. Her entire service was spent working both passenger and freight services until she was withdrawn from service whilst working from Carlisle Kingsmoor Shed in August 1965.

She was subsequently sold for scrap and spent two decades languishing in Woodham Brothers scrapyard until, in 1986, she was purchased by the British Rail Enginemen Society, who still own the locomotive. Since being purchased for preservation, 45293 was moved around before finding a permanent home on the Colne Valley Railway in 1996.

Restoration work has since been slow and intermittent but is still ongoing. No indication has been given as to when she will return to steam and she remains on the Colne Valley Railway.

4-6-0 LMS Stanier Class 5 (Black 5) Locomotive, No. 45428

Number 45428 was built by Armstrong Whitworth of Newcastle in October 1937 as LMS number 5428 (BR 45428). After spending some of her early years working at Carlisle and Manchester, 45428 was assigned to sheds in the Leeds area of West Yorkshire from 1955 onwards.

On 1 October 1967, 45428 hauled the last Bradford to London steam passenger express between Bradford and Leeds. She was withdrawn from service later that month. She remained in Leeds until 1968 when, after being purchased for preservation, she travelled to the Birmingham Railway Museum at Tyseley

Former LMS 4-6-0, Class 5 (Black 5) locomotive, number 45293, pictured at Carlisle Station whilst working a passenger train on 18 August 1964. *(© MC)*

Former LMS 4-6-0, Class 5 (Black 5) locomotive, number 45428, pictured at Leeds Holbeck Shed in 1967. (© PC)

for restoration. She remained there for a number of years and whilst at the museum, although previously un-named, she was given the name *Eric Treacy* after a former Bishop of Wakefield and an eminent railway photographer, who died in 1978.

Number 45428 later moved to the North Yorkshire Moors Railway, where she has since been based. She is fully operational on the NYMR, painted in her original LMS livery and bearing her LMS number 5428. She is owned by the North Yorkshire Railway Historical Railway Trust.

4-6-0 LMS Jubilee Class Locomotive, No. 45593 *Kolhapur*

Number 45593 was built by the North British Locomotive Company, Glasgow, in December 1934. She was originally unveiled in LMS crimson lake livery and allocated the number 5593. She was named *Kolhapur* after a princely state in Western India, which at that time was ruled by the British Raj. In December 1948, she was given her BR number 45593.

From September 1951, 45593 was assigned to Carlisle Upperby Shed where she worked for nine years until September 1960. She then worked out of six engine sheds in quick succession before being assigned to Leeds Holbeck in March 1965. Whilst there, she was given a yellow diagonal stripe on her cab-side which denoted that she was prohibited from working on the electrified West Coast Main Line, south of Crewe.

Former LMS 4-6-0, Jubilee Class locomotive, number 45593 *Kolhapur*, pictured working a rail tour at Pontefract Monkhill Station on 22 April 1967. *(© PC)*

Former LMS 4-6-0, Jubilee Class locomotive, number 45593 *Kolhapur*, pictured at Pontefract, West Yorkshire, in April 1967 whilst working a rail tour excursion train. *(© PC)*

During her time at Holbeck Shed, she was very well maintained and used primarily for working steam rail tours over the Settle and Carlisle railway line until she was withdrawn from service in October 1967.

After being withdrawn from service, 45593 was purchased for preservation by the then Standard Gauge Steam Trust (now 7029 Clun Castle Ltd) and moved to Tyseley Railway Museum in Birmingham. Restoration work was carried out and 45593 returned to service in 1985, adorned in her original LMS crimson lake livery and bearing her LMS number 5593.

She spent the next decade working numerous main line special excursion trains from her base at Tyseley and in 1995 she was repainted in BR Brunswick Green Livery, sporting her BR number 45593.

She continues to be based in Birmingham but is currently out of service awaiting an overhaul, which is due to commence sometime in 2020.

4-6-0 LMS Jubilee Class Locomotive, No. 45596 *Bahamas*

LMS Jubilee Class locomotives were designed by Sir William Stanier FRS, Chief Mechanical Engineer of the LMS Railway Company. The first locomotive of the class was named *Silver Jubilee*, hence the name Jubilee Class. The name was chosen to commemorate the Silver Jubilee of King George V, which took place in 1935. A total of 191 Jubilee Class locomotives were built between 1934 and 1936 for working main line passenger services.

Former LMS 4-6-0, Jubilee Class locomotive, number 45596 *Bahamas*, pictured working an up goods train at Hest Bank, Morecambe, on 18 August 1961. *(© PC)*

Number 45596 was built by the North British Locomotive Company, Glasgow, in January 1935 and was allocated LMS number 5596. She was given the name *Bahamas* after the group of islands in the West Atlantic Ocean which at the time were a part of the British Empire.

She was initially assigned to Crewe but operated out of a number of other sheds during her working life. In 1948, she was renumbered 45596 by BR after nationalisation took place.

In 1961, 45596 was fitted with a double blast pipe and chimney (see photograph) and the following year she was transferred from Carlisle to Stockport, from where she was withdrawn from service in July 1966.

After being withdrawn from service, 45596 was purchased for preservation by the Bahamas Locomotive Society

and transported to the Hunslet Engine Company in Leeds where she was restored to her former LMS livery. She re-entered service in 1968 and made visits to Stockport and Bury before moving to the Dinting Railway Museum Derbyshire which was to be her home for more than twenty years. She was on public display at the museum but could also be seen working a number of main line special excursion trains.

In 1989, 45596 was painted in BR Brunswick Green livery and moved to a new home at Ingrow on the Keighley and Worth Valley Railway after it was announced that the Dinting Museum was to close in 1991. Number 45596 is still in service, working on the Keighley & Worth Valley Railway, and in addition, since 2019 she has been operating special main line services for the first time since 1994.

Another photograph of former LMS 4-6-0, Jubilee Class locomotive, number 45596 *Bahamas*, pictured working an up parcels train at Hest Bank, Morecambe, on 24 August 1961. *(© PC)*

4-6-0 LMS Jubilee Class Locomotive, No. 45690 *Leander*

Number 45690 was built at Crewe in March 1936 and named after HMS *Leander*, a British Leander Class light cruiser commissioned in 1933. The locomotive *Leander* was allocated LMS number 5690 and assigned to Crewe North Shed until 1947 when she was transferred to Bristol Barrow Road from where she worked for the remainder of her service. She was renumbered 45690 by BR in 1948 and throughout the 1950s and early 1960s she frequently, and often daily, hauled passenger services between Bristol Temple Meads and the north-eastern cities of York and Newcastle via Birmingham and Sheffield, incurring heavy mileage.

After being withdrawn from service in July 1964, 45690 was sold for scrap and transported to Woodham Brothers in Barry, South Wales.

Number 45690 remained in Woodham Brothers scrapyard from July 1964 until May 1972, when she was bought for preservation by the late Mr Brian Oliver. She was transported to the BR Works in Derby where she was restored and put on display at the Dinting Railway Museum in Glossop, Derbyshire. In 1983, 45690 was sold to the Severn Valley Heritage Railway where she worked from 1984 until 1989, when she was put in storage in need of an overhaul. In 1994, 45690 was sold to the family of Dr Peter Beet. She was given an overhaul in 2012, before returning to service in 2014, painted in the BR lined black livery that she had carried between April 1949 and November 1952.

Number 45690 resumed her main line workings in 2015 and is still owned by the Beet family. She is currently based at the West Coast Railway Company in Carnforth. She is fully operational and main line certified.

A total of 191 LMS Jubilee Class locomotives were built between 1934 and 1936, to be used on main line passenger services. Five members of the class were built with double chimneys at various times to increase power and reduce coal consumption. Proposals were introduced in the 1940s for the entire class of Jubilee locomotives to be rebuilt with tapered

Former LMS 4-6-0 Jubilee Class locomotive, number 45690 *Leander*, pictured working a passenger train near Pontefract, West Yorkshire, in the late 1950s. (© PC)

Former LMS 4-6-0, Jubilee Class locomotive, number 45690 *Leander*, pictured working a Sheffield to Newcastle passenger train at Ackworth, West Yorkshire, on 6 June 1960. *(© PC)*

Former LMS 4-6-0, Jubilee Class locomotive, number 45690 *Leander,* working a York to Sheffield passenger train at Pontefract Baghill Station on 26 May 1959. *(© PC)*

Former LMS Jubilee Class locomotive, number 45690 *Leander,* pictured working a Bristol to Newcastle passenger train at Pontefract, West Yorkshire, on 8 November 1958. *(© PC)*

Former LMS Jubilee Class locomotive, number 45690 *Leander,* working a York to Bristol express through Pontefract, West Yorkshire, on 28 May 1959. *(© PC)*

Former LMS Jubilee Class locomotive, number 45690 *Leander,* working a Newcastle to Bristol passenger train at Pontefract, West Yorkshire, on 4 July 1959. (© *PC*)

Former LMS Jubilee Class locomotive, number 45690 *Leander,* working a Sheffield to York local passenger train near Pontefract Baghill Station in April 1958. (© *PC*)

boilers and double chimneys. Numbers 5735 *Comet* and 5736 *Phoenix* were the only two locomotives to receive the rebuild, after which the proposals were abandoned. Just four Jubilee Class locomotives (numbers 45593, 45596, 45690 and 45699) have been preserved.

4-6-0 LMS Jubilee Class Locomotive, No. 45699 *Galatea*

Number 45699 was built at Crewe in 1936 and allocated LMS number 5699. She was named after HMS *Galatea*, a British Arethusa Class light cruiser, commissioned in 1935. After entering service, the locomotive *Galatea* was assigned to Newton Heath Shed in Manchester. Number 45699 later worked on the LMS at Sheffield, Derby, Nottingham and Leeds.

After nationalisation in 1948, she was given her BR number, 45699 and transferred to Barrow Road Shed in Bristol, where she primarily worked long distance trains to the north-east of England via Birmingham and Sheffield throughout the 1950s. She moved to Shrewsbury in October 1961 before being withdrawn from service in November 1964. She was later sold for scrap and transported to Woodham Brothers scrapyard.

After being withdrawn from service, 45699 languished at Woodham Brothers until 1980, when she was rescued by the late Mr Brian Oliver and moved to the Severn Valley Railway, originally for the purpose of providing a boiler and other spare parts for her preserved sister locomotive number 45690 *Leander*, which was also owned by Mr Oliver.

In 1994, both 45699 *Galatea* and 45690 *Leander* were sold to the family of Doctor Peter Beet. Locomotive 45690 *Leander* was later restored on the East Lancashire Railway before moving to a new home at Carnforth to work main line special excursions and rail tours.

Number 45699 *Galatea* was initially moved to Tyseley in Birmingham

Former LMS **Jubilee** Class locomotive, number 45699 *Galatea* pictured at Bracken Hill Junction, Ackworth, West Yorkshire, on 14 May 1960 whilst working a Birmingham to Newcastle passenger train. (© PC)

Former LMS Jubilee Class locomotive, number 45699 *Galatea* pictured departing Pontefract Baghill Station, West Yorkshire, whilst working a Newcastle to Bristol express passenger train in 1957. *(© PC)*

Former LMS Jubilee Class locomotive, number 45699 *Galatea*, pictured working a Nottingham to Newcastle relief passenger train at Pontefract, West Yorkshire, on 3 August 1957. *(© PC)*

before being sold to the West Coast
Railway Company at Carnforth who
had offered to restore her in her own
right, rather than use her for spare parts.
After receiving a complete rebuild,
45699 returned to steam in April 2013
and joined her sister locomotive,
45690 *Leander*, in working steam specials
on the main line. Both locomotives are
currently operational.

4-6-0 LMS Royal Scot Class Locomotive, No. 46152 *Royal Scot*

Number 46100 was built at Derby in June
1930. In 1933, she visited Chicago and
made a tour of the main line railways
in the USA and Canada. The tour was a
huge success. Upon her return to Britain,

46100 spent her working life hauling
express passenger trains before being
withdrawn from service in 1962.

After being withdrawn from service,
46100 was purchased by Sir William 'Billy'
Butlin and put on display at his Skegness
holiday camp until 1972, when she moved
to Bressingham Steam Museum near Diss
in Norfolk.

In 2009, 46100 was sold to the Royal Scot
Locomotive & General Trust who are her
current owners. In 2015, 46100 visited the
Severn Valley Railway and in the spring
of 2017, she could be seen working on the
North Yorkshire Moors Railway. Number
46100 is currently based at Crewe from
where she works main line specials and
excursion trains.

Former LMS Royal Scot Class locomotive, 46100 *Royal Scot* pictured at Crewe Works on 8 May 1948, still in her LMS livery and bearing her LMS number 6100. There is little doubt that she was at the works awaiting repainting, as she emerged shortly afterwards repainted in BR Livery and displaying her new BR number. This photograph was taken before she was fitted with a 2A tapered boiler during a rebuild in 1950 (compare with engine number 46115 in the next picture). *(© PC)*

4-6-0 LMS Royal Scot Class Locomotive, No. 46115 *Scots Guardsman*

Number 46115 was built by the North British Locomotive Company at Glasgow in October 1927 as LMS number 6115 *Scots Guardsman*. She was fitted with smoke deflectors the following year. In 1936, 46115 featured in a famous cinema documentary film, entitled *Night Mail*, which focussed on the London to Glasgow, Royal Mail Travelling Post Office train.

Number 46115 was rebuilt in 1947 and worked for BR until being withdrawn from service at Carlisle in December 1965. She was later purchased for preservation and moved to the Keighley & Worth Valley Railway but she was found to be too large for their requirements at that particular time. She then went through changes of ownership until she was eventually purchased by Mr David Smith, owner of the West Coast Railway Company, who gave her a full restoration that was completed in 2008.

Number 46115 has since worked main line excursions and rail tours, usually from her home base at the West Coast Railway Company in Carnforth. She was also chosen to carry the Olympic Torch for the 2012 Olympic Games which were held in London. Number 46115 is expected to continue working on the main line for a number of years.

Former LMS **Royal** Scot Class locomotive, number 46115 *Scots Guardsman* pictured at Crewe in 1961. She is fitted with a tapered boiler which she received during a rebuild in 1947. (© PC)

4-6-2 LMS Coronation Class Locomotive, No. 46235 *City of Birmingham*

Number 46235 was built at Crewe in July 1939 as a streamlined locomotive, LMS number 6235. She was the first of her class to be fitted with a double chimney. Her streamlined casing was removed in April 1946 for maintenance reasons and replaced by smoke deflectors.

She was painted black during the war years and then in an experimental BR blue livery in 1950. This blue livery was discontinued shortly afterwards and 46235 was repainted BR Brunswick Green in April 1953. She continued working express passenger trains until she was withdrawn from service at Crewe in 1964.

Number 46235 was subsequently preserved as a part of the national

Former LMS **Coronation** Class locomotive, number 46235 *City of Birmingham*, pictured departing Rugby with a passenger train on 8 August 1962. (© PC)

collection and exhibited at the Birmingham Museum of Science and Industry. She was a star attraction at the museum. The museum closed in 1997 but was replaced in 2001 by the new Thinktank Birmingham Science Museum.

Number 46235 *City of Birmingham* is now preserved for posterity and can be seen proudly on public display at the Thinktank Museum in Birmingham, the city after which she was named.

2-6-0 LMS (2F) Design (BR Built) Class 2MT Locomotive, No. 46443

Number 46443 was built at Crewe in February 1949 as a mixed traffic locomotive (Classifications: LMS 2F, BR 2MT). She was initially assigned to Derby Shed, from where she worked local passenger services between Nottingham,

Derby and Birmingham. She moved to Saltley, Birmingham in 1961 to work commuter passenger trains, before being transferred to Newton Heath in Manchester in 1966. She was withdrawn from service in March 1967.

After being withdrawn, she was purchased from BR for preservation by Mr Richard Willcox, to be used on the newly formed Severn Valley Heritage Railway. The railway officially opened in 1970 and 46443 played an important role in the opening ceremony. The SVR later bought 46443 and she earned the nickname 'The People's Engine' due to her popularity.

Number 46443 continues to be based on the Severn Valley Railway and is the longest serving member of their entire locomotive fleet.

Former LMS Class 2F locomotive, number 46443, pictured at Shirebrook North in Derbyshire on 3 July 1954, whilst working a Stephenson Locomotive Society rail tour. *(© PC)*

2-6-0 LMS (2F) Design (BR Built) Class 2MT Locomotive, No. 46512

(Named *E V Cooper Engineer* during preservation.)

Number 46512 was built by BR at Swindon works in December 1952 from an LMS Ivatt (2F) design. She was built primarily to work on the Western Region of BR and assigned to Oswestry. She was withdrawn from service whilst working out of Crewe South Shed in December 1966.

After being withdrawn, 46512 was sold for scrap and languished in Woodham Brothers scrapyard until May 1973, when she was purchased for preservation by the Highland Locomotive Company and transported to the Strathspey Heritage Railway at Aviemore in the Scottish Highlands.

Number 46512 was painstakingly restored under the directions of an engineer, Mr E.V. Cooper, and was later named after him. She continues to work on the Strathspey Railway.

0-6-0T LMS Fowler Jinty Class 3F Tank Locomotive, No. 47406

Number 47406 was built in December 1926 by the Vulcan Foundry Locomotive Works at Newton-le-Willows, Merseyside in Lancashire, as LMS number 16489. She later became LMS 7406 and BR 47406.

In 1928, 47406 was assigned to Carnforth Shed where she performed freight duties for over thirty years. Her last six years were spent at Warrington, Manchester and Liverpool, from where she was withdrawn from service in December 1966.

Former LMS design Class 2 light mixed traffic locomotive, number 46512, pictured at Oswestry Station on 24 April 1963 about to work a passenger train along the branch line from Oswestry to Llanfyllin. The branch line was closed in 1965 as a consequence of the Beeching report and 46512 worked the last passenger train along the line on 17 January 1965. (© PC)

LMS Class 3F Jinty tank locomotive, number 47406, pictured on freight duties at Carnforth, Lancashire, on 26 April 1947 before the railways were nationalised. She is in her LMS livery and bearing LMS number 7406. *(© PC)*

Number 47406 was sold for scrap and transported to Woodham Brothers scrapyard where she remained until 1983, when she was purchased for preservation by the Rowsley Locomotive Trust, who transported her to Peak Rail Headquarters at Buxton in Derbyshire.

In 1989, 47406 was sold to Mr Roger Hibbert for use on the Great Central Heritage Railway. She was stored at Loughborough until restoration work could be carried out.

In January 2010, 47406 was successfully restored to steam and has since continued to work on the Great Central Heritage Railway.

2-8-0 LMS (S&DR) Class 7F Locomotive, No. 53808

Number 53808 was built by Robert Stephenson & Company Locomotive Works at Darlington in July 1925 as Somerset & Dorset Railway locomotive number 88. She was painted in black unlined livery and assigned to Bath Green Park Engine Shed where she remained for almost forty years, before being withdrawn from service in 1964.

Number 53808 spent most of her life on the former Somerset & Dorset Railway, working local goods trains on the steep inclines of the Mendip Hills between Bath and Evercreech Junction. During the 1950s

Former LMS (S&DR) Class 7F, number 53808, pictured at Derby Motive Power Depot on 14 August 1949, fitted with a large Stephenson design boiler (5.3 in / 160 cm) which she received when she was built in 1925. Although in her new BR livery and displaying her BR number, she still bears her old LMS shed plate, number 22C (Bath). *(© PC)*

however, she could be seen hauling some of the many summer holiday passenger trains (mainly from the Midlands and the North) between Bath and the south coast holiday resort of Bournemouth.

In 1930, S&DR locomotives were absorbed into LMS stock and number 88 became LMS number 9678. In 1932 she was renumbered LMS 13808 before receiving her BR number 53808 after nationalisation.

A comparison of the two photographs reveals the difference between the original

Fowler boiler and the larger Stephenson boiler which was fitted to 53808 when she was built. A total of five locomotives, all built in 1925, were fitted with Stephenson boilers, to assist them in working heavy mineral trains on the steep inclines of the Mendip hills on the S & DR. All five of these locomotives (including 53808) were later rebuilt with the standard (but smaller) Fowler boilers.

After being withdrawn from service, 53808 was sold for scrap but later

Former LMS (S&DR) Class 7F number 53808, pictured at Templecombe Shed on 11 May 1958. In this picture, she is fitted with an original SDJR, 7F Fowler design, boiler (4.9 in / 145 cm) introduced in 1914, which she received during a rebuild in 1954. *(Photo© PC)*

Former LMS (S&DR) Class 7F number 53808, pictured at Templecombe on 11 September 1960. In this photograph, 53808 is hauling two brake-vans on the former Somerset & Dorset Railway. It is likely that she was taking the brake-vans to Radstock, which is situated in the former Somerset Coalfield, to pick up and transport a northbound coal train towards Bath. *(© PC)*

purchased from Woodham Brothers by the Somerset and Dorset Railway Trust. In 1976, 53808 was transported to the West Somerset Heritage Railway where restoration was carried out.

After being preserved, 53808 returned to steam in August 1987 painted in unlined black livery and displaying an early 1950s BR crest. Further overhauls were carried out in 1996 and 2014. In December 2005, she was repainted in Somerset & Dorset Joint Railway blue livery and sporting her S&DJR number 88.

In reality, she was never painted blue whilst in service as she was painted black from the time she began working in 1925. In February 2016, 53808 was again repainted black but on this occasion she displayed a late 1950s BR Crest, which remains unchanged. She continues to work on the West Somerset Heritage Railway, where she is expected to remain.

Former LMS (LNWR) (NLR) locomotive, number 58850, pictured whilst performing shunting duties at Cromford, on the Cromford and High Peak railway line in Derbyshire in the early 1950s. (© PC)

0-6-0T LMS (LNWR) (NLR) Class 2F Locomotive, No. 58850

A total of thirty of these powerful 0-6-0 tank locomotives were built as Class 75 locomotives for the North London Railway between 1879 and 1905. They were designed and built for use as shunting engines at the East India and West India Docks in London.

Number 58850 was built at the North London Railway Locomotive Works, Bow, east London, in 1880 and allocated NLR number 76. She was re-numbered 116 in 1891 before being rebuilt in 1897. In 1909, she went into the stock of the LNWR as locomotive number 2650. The LNWR was absorbed into the LMS Railway in 1923, and in 1926 she was given the LMS number 7505. In 1934 she was renumbered LMS 27505 and her final number, 58850, was allocated by BR in 1949.

During the 1930s, 58850 was assigned to Rowsley Shed in Derbyshire, which served

the Cromford and High Peak railway line. She spent the remainder of her working life there, hauling freight trains along the steep gradients, as well as carrying out shunting duties. She ceased working at Rowsley in May 1960 and was mothballed until being officially withdrawn from service in September 1960. Number 58850 was the last locomotive in the class to be withdrawn from BR service and the only one subsequently preserved.

After being withdrawn, 58850 was stored at Derby until 1962 when, still in good working order, she was sold to the Bluebell Heritage Railway for the sum of £890. After working for a number of years on the Bluebell line, it was discovered that 58850 was in need of major boiler

work and an overhaul. She was taken out of service and loaned out to various institutions to be put on public display.

In October 2005, 58850 returned to the Bluebell Railway and has been on static display at Sheffield Park ever since. It is anticipated that she will remain on display until she receives her much needed overhaul. No indication has been given as to when this will be carried out, or when she will be back in service.

0-6-2T LMS (LNWR) Class 2F (Webb Coal Tank) Locomotive, No. 58926

Number 58926 was built at Crewe in September 1888 and given LNWR number 1054. A total of 300 of these engines were built and generally became known as 'coal

Former LMS (LNWR) (NLR) locomotive, number 58850, pictured on the High Peak railway line in Derbyshire circa 1949. *(© PC)*

tanks'. After working in the midlands, 58926 was transferred to Abergavenny in 1919, where she worked the former LNWR line to Merthyr Tydfil until the late 1930s. She was allocated LMS number 7799 in 1926.

She later worked from various sheds and was allocated her BR number, 58926, in 1949. In 1954 she spent some time on loan to the National Coal Board before returning to BR at Abergavenny. She moved to Pontypool Road Shed in January 1958 and was withdrawn from service in October of that year.

After being withdrawn from service, 58926 was moved to Crewe to be scrapped by BR. As she awaited her final disposal, Mr J.M. Dunn, former Shed Master at Bangor, organised a Webb Coal Tank Engine Preservation Fund and within six months she was purchased for preservation. She was subsequently repainted in her former LNWR livery and transported to Hednesford in Staffordshire, where she was placed in storage by the Railway Preservation Society.

In 1963, ownership of 58926 was transferred to the National Trust who continue to own her. Since 1963, 58926 has visited various locations but is now based on the Keighley & Worth Valley Railway at the Ingrow Locomotive Works. She is fully operational and regularly working on the K&WVR. Number 58926 is maintained by the Bahamas Locomotive Society on behalf of the National Trust.

In November 2019, number 58926 was taken out of service due to defective boiler tubes. It is hoped that the repairs can be carried out for her to return to steam in time for a centenary to commemorate the 1922 Amalgamation of the L & YR with the LNWR which is due to take place in January 2022.

Former LMS (LNWR) tank locomotive, number 58926, pictured at Merthyr Tydfil on Saturday, 6 January 1958. The previous day, Sunday, 5 January, she was the front locomotive of a double header which worked the last passenger train from Abergavenny to Merthyr on the former LNWR Abergavenny to Merthyr Tydfil railway line. The train was a special excursion train, organised by the Stephenson Locomotive Society. The last service passenger train had run the day before (Saturday, 4 January 1958). *(© PC)*

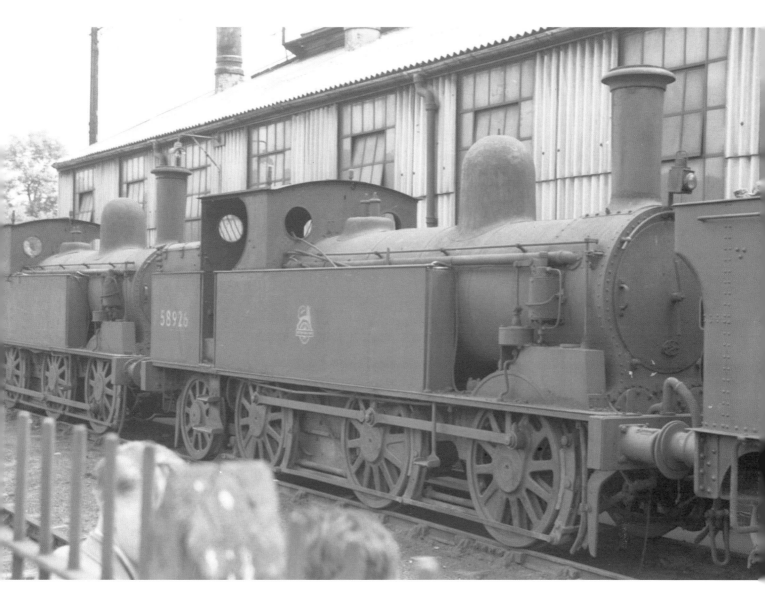

Former LMS (LNWR) tank locomotive, number 58926, pictured at Abercynon in South Wales on 26 June 1955, whilst on a short term loan from BR to the National Coal Board. *(© PC)*

CHAPTER 4

LNER – LONDON AND NORTH EASTERN RAILWAY LOCOMOTIVES

Former LNER Class A4 locomotive, number 60007 *Sir Nigel Gresley* pictured working a Leeds to King's Cross passenger express at Moorhouse near South Elmsall, West Yorkshire, on 23 April 1962. (© PC)

4-6-2 LNER Class A4 Locomotive, No. 60007 *Sir Nigel Gresley*

Number 60007 was built at Doncaster in October 1937 and entered service in LNER Garter Blue livery, bearing LNER number 4498. In 1946, she was renumbered LNER number 7.

She was given the name *Sir Nigel Gresley* at an official naming ceremony which took place at Marylebone Station in London in November 1937. The locomotive was originally due to have been named *Bittern* until it was realised that she was the 100th Pacific Locomotive designed by Sir Nigel Gresley to have been built. Consequently it was decided to name the locomotive after him. The name *Bittern* was later bestowed upon another Class A4 locomotive, LNER 4464.

From February 1942 until March 1947, she was painted wartime black then she was renumbered 60007 by BR after 1948.

In 1950 she was painted dark blue and in April 1952 she was repainted BR

Former LNER Class A4 locomotive, number 60007 *Sir Nigel Gresley*, pictured at Brayton near Selby, North Yorkshire, on 6 July 1963, whilst working a Mallard Commemorative Silver Jubilee Special rail tour. *(© PC)*

Former LNER Class A4 locomotive, number 60007 *Sir Nigel Gresley*, pictured working a down express though Thirsk, North Yorkshire, on 10 April 1962. *(© PC)*

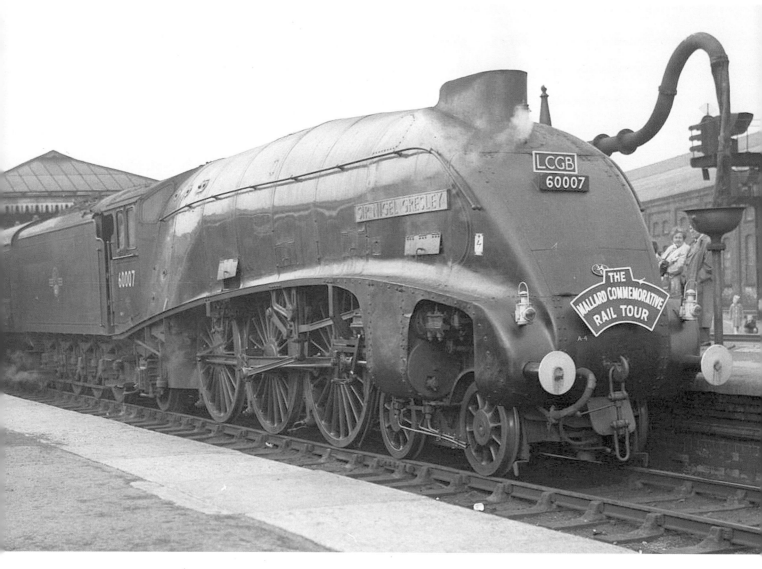

Former LNER Class A4 locomotive, number 60007 *Sir Nigel Gresley*, pictured at York Station on 6 July 1963, whilst working a Mallard Commemorative Silver Jubilee Special rail tour. (© PC)

Brunswick Green, which she retained until she was withdrawn from service whilst working out of Ferryhill Shed, Aberdeen, in February 1966. Number 60007 spent most of her service assigned to King's Cross Top Shed in London and worked East Coast Main Line passenger services from London to Leeds, York, Newcastle and Edinburgh. Her last three years were spent in Scotland working express services between Aberdeen and Glasgow.

After being withdrawn from service in 1966, 60007 was saved from the scrapyard by the A4 Preservation Society. She is currently owned by the Sir Nigel Gresley Locomotive Trust Ltd and works on the North Yorkshire Moors Railway where she is based.

It is a well-known fact that a sister A4 Class locomotive number 60022 (LNER 4468) *Mallard* holds the world steam speed record of 126 mph (203 km/h); however, 60007 does in fact hold the official post-war world steam speed record of 112 mph (180 km/h), which she set on 23 May 1959 whilst hauling a train full of passengers on a Stephenson Locomotive Society rail tour at Stoke Bank, Lincolnshire, on the East Coast Main Line. A plaque was later affixed to the locomotive to mark the event.

4-6-2 LNER Class A4 Locomotive, No. 60008 *Dwight D. Eisenhower*

Number 60008 was built at Doncaster in September 1937 as LNER number 4496. She was originally named *Golden Shuttle*

but was renamed *Dwight D. Eisenhower* after the Second World War. She spent her LNER and BR service working express passenger trains on the East Coast Main Line.

Number 60008 was withdrawn from service in July 1963 and earmarked by British Railways for preservation. She was later gifted to the United States of America. Number 60008 was subsequently shipped to America in May 1964 and transported to the National Railroad Museum in Ashwaubenon, Wisconsin, USA.

In 2012, 60008 returned to Britain as part of the plans to unite all six preserved Class A4 locomotives to mark the 75th Anniversary of the world steam speed

record-breaking run. In 2013, 60008 was exhibited in the National Railway Museum in York before returning to the USA in 2014.

She remains on public display at the US National Railroad Museum.

4-6-2 LNER Class A4 Locomotive, No. 60009 *Union of South Africa*

Number 60009 was built at Doncaster in June 1937 and numbered LNER 4488. She was originally allocated the name *Osprey* in April 1937, but when she entered service on 29 June she had been renamed *Union of South Africa* as a result of the country becoming a Sovereign Dominion of the British Empire in December 1931. In 1961, the country became the Republic of South Africa after leaving the British Commonwealth.

Former LNER Class A4 locomotive, number 60008 *Dwight D. Eisenhower* pictured at Selby in North Yorkshire hauling the London King's Cross to Newcastle down *Norseman* express passenger train on 28 August 1961. *(© PC)*

Former LNER Class A4 locomotive number 60009 *Union of South Africa*, pictured at Selby Station, North Yorkshire, hauling *The Elizabethan* King's Cross to Aberdeen down express passenger train on 22 August 1961. (© PC)

She entered service in 1937 painted in LNER Garter Blue livery and numbered 4488. Upon entering service, she was assigned to Edinburgh Haymarket Shed to work express passenger trains on the East Coast Main Line, before being transferred to Aberdeen (Ferryhill) in May 1962 to work passenger services to Glasgow.

In 1942, her original streamlined valances were removed for ease of maintenance and, like other locomotives during the Second World War, she was painted austere black. Her streamlined valances were never replaced. In1946, number 60009 was re-numbered LNER number nine and she reverted back to her original garter blue livery the following year. She received her BR number, 60009 after the railways were nationalised in 1948.

In August 1949, 60009 was repainted in a new BR experimental blue livery but the colour was discontinued some two years later. Finally, in October 1952, she was turned out in British Railways Brunswick Green livery which she retained for the rest of her service and throughout her subsequent years in preservation. She was withdrawn from service in June 1966.

After being withdrawn from service, 60009 was purchased for preservation by Mr John Cameron, a Scottish farmer, who initially based her on the Lochty Private Railway in Fife, Scotland, but the railway later closed and 60009 was put to work on the main line network.

Former LNER Class A4 locomotive, number 60009 *Union of South Africa*, pictured hauling *The Elizabethan* Aberdeen to King's Cross (non-stop from Edinburgh) express passenger train through Selby in North Yorkshire on 1 August 1961. *(© PC)*

Former LNER Class A4 locomotive, number 60009 *Union of South Africa*, pictured at Selby, North Yorkshire, on 24 October 1964 whilst hauling a Stephenson Locomotive Society Special rail tour, *The Jubilee Requiem,* from London King's Cross to Newcastle and return. *(© PC)*

Since 1972, 60009 has spent over forty years working main line special excursion trains to numerous destinations nationwide, incurring heavy mileage. She has also visited a number of Heritage Railways. During part of the 1980s and 1990s, whilst in preservation, 60009 reverted to the name *Osprey* during a period of political tensions and civil unrest which was taking place in South Africa at the time.

Number 60009 will continue operating during 2020 before being taken out of service in need of an overhaul. After that, her future is uncertain, but Mr Cameron is considering building a museum on his farm in Fife, Scotland, to exhibit 60009 and LNER Class K4 locomotive 61994, which he also owns.

Former LNER Class A4 locomotive, number 60010 *Dominion of Canada*, pictured as a light engine at Doncaster Shed in May 1951. *(© PC)*

4-6-2 LNER Class A4 Locomotive, No. 60010 *Dominion of Canada*

A total of thirty-five Class A4 locomotives were introduced to the LNER between 1935 and 1938. Number 60010 was built at Doncaster in May 1937 as LNER number 4489. Initially she was allocated the name *Buzzard* but instead was named *Woodcock*. The following month she saw a further name change when she was renamed *Dominion of Canada*. She was later presented with a Canadian Pacific Railway locomotive bell by the Canadian Pacific Railway Company. The bell, which was steam operated, was fitted in front of the chimney and used on a number of occasions. In addition, they provided her with a Canadian Pacific Railway issue 5-chime whistle which was also

Former LNER Class A4 locomotive, number 60010 *Dominion of Canada,* pictured at King Edwards Bridge, Newcastle, hauling the down *Flying Scotsman* train during the mid-1950s. The locomotive is sporting a genuine Canadian Pacific Railway bell & whistle. *(© PC)*

Former LNER Class A4 locomotive, number 60010 *Dominion of Canada,* pictured at Moss in South Yorkshire, hauling the up *Flying Scotsman* express passenger train (Edinburgh to King's Cross) on 25 June 1960. *(© PC)*

Former LNER Class A4 locomotive, number 60010 *Dominion of Canada*, pictured working a passenger train through Low Moor, Bradford, on 19 November 1961. *(© PC)*

fitted to the locomotive. Both items were removed in 1958. In May 1946, 60010 was renumbered LNER number 10, then given her BR number 60010 after the railways were nationalised in 1948.

Number 60010 was designed to work express passenger services. Upon entering service, she was assigned to King's Cross Top Shed where, apart from a six months spell at Grantham in 1957, she worked the next twenty-six years, hauling express passenger trains out of London King's Cross to Scotland and the north-east of England on the East Coast Main Line.

1963 saw steam locomotives being replaced by Deltic Diesel Electric locomotives on the East Coast Main Line and 60010 was transferred to Peterborough where she spent a mere four months before

being moved to Ferryhill Locomotive Shed in Aberdeen, Scotland. She spent the remainder of her working life on BR, operating express passenger services between Aberdeen and Glasgow until she was withdrawn from service on 29 May 1965.

After being withdrawn from service, 60010 was moved to Darlington and her records were endorsed to be sold for scrap. She subsequently languished in a siding at Darlington Shed, almost forgotten.

Darlington Shed closed in 1966 and 60010 was moved to Crewe where it was decided that British Rail would donate 60010 to the Canadian Railroad Historical Association.

After some restoration, 60010 was shipped to Canada and preserved at the

Canadian Railway Museum in Quebec. She visited Britain between 2012 and 2014 for the Mallard 75 Year Speed event. Upon arrival in the UK, she was restored to her original LNER Garter Blue livery and given her LNER number 4489, before being put on public display inside York Railway Museum.

In June 2014 she was shipped home and is now back on display at the Canadian Railway Museum at Saint-Constant, Delson, Quebec in Canada.

4-6-2 LNER Class A4 Locomotive, No. 60019 *Bittern*

Number 60019 was built at Doncaster in December 1937 as LNER number 4464. She became LNER number 19 in 1946 and BR 60019 in 1948. She spent almost

her entire life with the LNER and BR, based at Newcastle and Gateshead from where she worked East Coast Main Line express passenger services between London, the north-east of England and Scotland.

During the war years, like other Class A4 locomotives, 60019 was painted in wartime black livery. Her streamlined valances which she was originally fitted with were removed for ease of maintenance but were never replaced. From Gateshead, 60019 worked wartime passenger services and also heavy coal trains which she was never designed for. After the war, she returned to the East Coast Main Line to work the express passenger services which she was designed to work.

LNER Class A4 locomotive, number 60010 *Dominion of Canada*, pictured working a King's Cross to Leeds passenger train at Beeston near Leeds, circa 1947. She is in her LNER livery and bearing her LNER number 10. The Canadian Pacific Railway bell is clearly visible in front of the chimney. The bell was later removed to allow a double chimney to be fitted in 1958. (© PC)

Former LNER Class A4 locomotive, number 60019 *Bittern*, pictured hauling an Anglo–Scottish car-carrier through Moss in South Yorkshire on 4 June 1960. (© PC)

Number 60019 spent her final years with BR at Ferryhill Shed in Aberdeen. From there, she worked express passenger trains between Aberdeen and Glasgow from the winter of 1963 until she was withdrawn from service on 5 September 1966. She was the last Class A4 locomotive to work the Aberdeen to Glasgow service.

After being withdrawn from service, 60019 was purchased privately and operated a number of main line charter trains from York before being taken out of service for overhaul.

Later, 60019 was put on display at the Dinting Railway Centre in Glossop, Derbyshire until 1987. She went through a change of ownership in 1995 before being purchased by her current owner Mr Jeremy Hosking in 2000. He moved her to the Mid Hants Heritage Railway for further restoration in 2001, and in May 2007, with her restoration complete, she returned to steam painted in BR lined green livery. She has since worked a number of main line charter trains and special excursions.

In June 2018, 60019 was taken out of service in need of a further overhaul. She was placed into storage at Margate, Kent, having joined a queue of other locomotives awaiting overhauls at the LNWR Heritage Centre in Crewe. After the work has been carried out, she is expected to return to work on the Mid Hants Railway as well as resuming her duties on the main line network.

4-6-2 LNER Class A4 Locomotive, No. 60022 *Mallard*

Number 60022 was built at Doncaster in March 1938 and entered service as LNER number 4468, bearing the name *Mallard* (named after a wild duck). She was renumbered LNER 22 in March 1948 and BR 60022 in 1949.

Number 60022 will be remembered for an event which took place on Sunday, 3 July 1938, when *Mallard* officially broke the unsurpassed world speed record for a steam locomotive, after attaining a speed of 126 mph (202.7 km/h) whilst travelling on a slight downward gradient at Stoke Bank just south of Grantham, in Lincolnshire, on the East Coast Main Line, whilst hauling a dynamometer car and six passenger coaches.

Upon entering service, 60022 was assigned to Doncaster Shed to work express passenger services, before being transferred to Grantham Shed in October 1943. After the railways were nationalised in 1948, 60022 was moved to King's Cross Top Shed in London and she spent her entire BR service working express passenger trains on the East Coast Main Line between London, the north-east of England and Scotland.

Former LNER Class A4 locomotive, number 60019 *Bittern*, pictured at York Railway Station working a King's Cross to Newcastle express passenger train in the early 1950s. A young boy is running along the platform clutching his camera, no doubt eager to capture his all-important photograph before the train departs. (© *PC*)

Former LNER Class A4 Pacific locomotive number 60022 *Mallard*, pictured hauling an up Anglo–Scottish car carrier through Moss in South Yorkshire on 25 June 1960. *(© PC)*

Former LNER Class A4 Pacific locomotive number 60022 *Mallard*, pictured on 26 August 1960, speeding non-stop through Selby in North Yorkshire whilst working the down *Flying Scotsman* express passenger train, the 10 am, London King's Cross to Edinburgh, Waverley. *(© PC)*

Number 60022 was withdrawn from service on 25 April 1963 and preserved as a part of the National Collection.

After being withdrawn from service, 60022 was taken to Doncaster where she was restored to her original LNER condition. Her streamlined valances, which had been removed in 1942, were replaced by replicas. She was painted in her original LNER Garter Blue livery, sporting her original number 4468 and her name *Mallard*. She was later hauled by rail to Nine Elms in South London, before being transported by road to the Museum of British Transport at Clapham, where she was put on public display. In 1975, after over a decade, 60022 was transported to her permanent home at the National Railway Museum in York.

During the 1980s, 60022 made several runs on the main line network. Her last outing was in August 1988, after which, she was taken out of service for further restoration.

Number 60022 has since been on public display in the main hall at the National Railway Museum in York, where she is a star attraction amongst the many thousands of visitors.

4-6-2 LNER Class A3 Locomotive, No. 60103 *Flying Scotsman*

The LNER Company was established on 1 January 1923. A few weeks later, the company acquired its first new build locomotive, a GNR design, Class A1 Pacific, which left Doncaster Works on 24 February 1923 displaying GNR number 1472. She was later re-numbered LNER 4472 and given the name *Flying Scotsman*, after an LNER passenger train bearing that name. The train operated between London King's Cross and Edinburgh Waverley in both directions. The down-service from King's Cross, and the up-service from Edinburgh, both departed at 10 am daily. The *Flying Scotsman* train service had been operating since 1862.

Former LNER Class A3 locomotive number, 60103 *Flying Scotsman*, pictured at Ardsley, South Yorkshire, working the down *Queen of Scots* in June 1962. She is fitted with German design Witte wind deflecting plates (smoke deflectors) which she received in December 1961. (© *PC*)

She was renumbered LNER 503 in January 1946 followed by LNER 103 just four months later. After nationalisation in 1948 she ran as BR number E103 until she was allocated BR number 60103 in 1949.

In 1924 and 1925, *Flying Scotsman* received some distinction when she was exhibited at the British Empire Exhibitions held at Wembley. Her main claim to fame however, occurred several years later, when, on 30 November 1934, whilst on a special test run, she was recorded as travelling at a speed of 100 mph (160.934 km/h) and was formally credited as being the first British locomotive to have officially reached that speed. She was converted from a Class A1 to a Class A3 locomotive in 1947.

A total of fifty-two Class A1 locomotives were built for the LNER between 1922 and 1935. All but one were later rebuilt as Class A3 locomotives. In addition, a further twenty-seven new Class A3 locomotives were built, taking the grand total of Class A3 locomotives produced, to seventy-nine. Sadly, number 60103, *Flying Scotsman* is the sole survivor of the class, after being purchased privately from BR for preservation.

She was converted to a Class A3 locomotive in January 1947 and the following year she was taken into the stock of locomotives under the control of the newly formed British Railways (BR). She was allocated the BR number 60103 and in 1950 she left her familiar territory of the East Coast Main Line and moved to Leicester from where she worked passenger services on the former Great Central Railway main line between Nottingham Victoria and London Marylebone. The main line which ran from London Marylebone to Manchester London Road (renamed Manchester Piccadilly in 1960) via Leicester, Nottingham, and Sheffield Victoria (closed 1970), was closed by virtue of the Beeching Report in the mid-1960s.

Former LNER Class
A3 locomotive number 60103 *Flying Scotsman*, fitted with Witte smoke deflectors, pictured at Leeds Central Station in June 1962. Leeds Central Station closed in 1967.
(© PC)

In November 1953, 60103 moved back to her roots on the East Coast Main Line and spent the last decade of her service with BR working out of Grantham and King's Cross until being withdrawn from service in 1963.

Number 60103 was withdrawn from service at King's Cross on 15 January 1963 and bought directly from BR for preservation by the entrepreneur Mr Alan Pegler. She was later restored to her original LNER condition and worked a number of main line rail tours for steam enthusiasts.

In 1969, Mr Pegler decided to take his locomotive on a tour of America and Canada. The tour was a partial success but the huge costs incurred resulted in 60103 being stranded in a US Army Depot near San Francisco with no funds available to return her home.

In 1973, British Businessman Sir William McAlpine bought her and returned her to Carnforth in the UK. She then went through several changes of ownership and visited Australia before going on sale again in 2004.

This time a successful campaign was launched, spearheaded by the National Railway Museum, to save 60103 *Flying Scotsman* for the nation and she was later purchased by the NRM. She returned to steam in 2016 to work main line specials. The NRM have announced that 60103 will continue in service until 2022, when she will be given an overhaul prior to special events being held to celebrate her centenary in 2023. In addition, the NRM have also announced that *Flying Scotsman* will be main line certified until 2029, after which, she will spend the next three years working on heritage railways.

Former LNER Class A3 locomotive number 60103 *Flying Scotsman*, pictured at Selby, North Yorkshire, hauling the King's Cross to Newcastle down *Norseman* on 17 August 1961. This photograph was taken before she was fitted with the Witte smoke deflectors. *(© PC)*

4-6-0 LNER Design (BR Built) Class B1 Locomotive, No. 61306

Former LNER design, Class B1 locomotive, number 61306, was built by the North British Locomotive Works at Glasgow as LNER number 1306, although she never actually displayed that number. She entered service in April 1948, shortly after nationalisation, painted in LNER Apple Green livery and displaying her new BR number 61306. The words BRITISH RAILWAYS were painted on the sides of the tender.

She spent the whole of her life working out of Hull, apart from her last few months, when she was moved to Low Moor Shed in Bradford until being withdrawn from service in September 1967.

In February 1968, 61306 was bought privately from BR and taken to 'Steamtown', Carnforth where she was restored in LNER Apple Green livery.

She displayed her original LNER number, 1306, which she never used whilst in service. She was also given the name *Mayflower* which had previously been used on a sister Class B1 locomotive number 61379, which was scrapped in August 1962. Number 61306 remained in Carnforth until 1978, when she moved to the Great Central Heritage Railway.

In the years that followed, 61306 went through changes of ownership and moved locations which included the Nene Valley Railway and the West Coast Railways at Carnforth. Number 61306 is currently based on the North Norfolk Railway. She is main line certified, having worked her first main line service in February 2019. She is expected to remain on the North Norfolk Railway for the foreseeable future and continue main line workings under the watchful eye of her current owner, Mr David Buck.

Former LNER design Class B1 locomotive, number 61306, pictured near Knottingley, West Yorkshire, whilst working a Hull rugby league football special on 15 April 1961. *(© PC)*

Former LNER design, Class B1 locomotive, number 61306, pictured at Castleford, West Yorkshire, working a Castleford to Leeds rugby football special in 1959. *(© PC)*

Former LNER design, Class B1 locomotive, number 61306, pictured hauling the *Scarborough Flyer* at Scarborough on 5 September 1959. *(© PC)*

2-6-0 LNER Design (BR Built) Class K1 Locomotive, No. 62005

(Since being preserved, displays the name *Lord of the Isles* during the summer season.)

Number 62005 was built by the North British Locomotive Company in Glasgow and entered service with BR in June 1949. Upon entering service, she was assigned to Darlington Shed and spent her entire service working in the north-east of England.

A total of seventy Class K1 locomotives were built and were the last LNER design locomotives ever built. None of these engines actually worked for the LNER as they were all built in Glasgow between May 1949 and March 1950, after nationalisation had taken place.

These Class K1 locomotives were efficient two-cylinder, mixed traffic locomotives (6 MT), which worked primarily in the east and north-east of England as well as in Scotland. Number

62005 was the last remaining Class K1 locomotive when she was withdrawn from service whilst working out of Leeds Holbeck Shed on 31 December 1967. She is the only Class K1 locomotive to have been preserved.

After being withdrawn from service, 62005 was purchased by a private consortium to be used primarily as a spare boiler source for the already preserved LNER Class K4 locomotive, number 61994, *The Great Marquess*, which was being stored at Leeds Neville Hill Depot. Locomotive 62005 was also taken to Neville Hill and stored alongside her. In 1972, it was decided that her boiler was no longer required for the K4 locomotive, so 62005 was donated to the North Eastern Locomotive Preservation Group to be preserved in her own right.

Number 62005 was later fully restored and main line certified before being moved to the NYMR in 1974.

Former LNER design, Class K1 locomotive, number 62005, pictured hauling a down goods train on the Sheffield to York line near Pontefract Baghill Station on 14 April 1961. (© PC)

She has remained there ever since. She regularly spends the summer months working the *Jacobite* passenger train service along the West Highland line in Scotland where she displays the name *Lord of the Isles,* which was formerly allocated to LNER Class K4 locomotive number 61996 (LNER number 3443) which worked the West Highland line displaying the name until being withdrawn from service in 1961 (scrapped in 1962).

4-4-0 LNER (GNSC) Class D40 Locomotive, No. 62277 *Gordon Highlander*

Number 62277 was built by the North British Locomotive Works, Glasgow, in 1920 for the Great North of Scotland

Railway. She was designated a Class F locomotive, number 49 and named *Gordon Highlander* after the Scottish Infantry Regiment. She initially hauled express passenger trains before working as a mixed traffic locomotive in her later years.

After the 1923 railway groupings, 62277 became an LNER Class D40, number 6849. She was later re-numbered LNER 2277 and BR 62277. She spent all her working life in Scotland and was the last working locomotive of her class when she was withdrawn from service in June 1958.

After being withdrawn, 62277 was preserved and restored at Inverurie Works, Aberdeen. She was painted in GNSR Green livery, bearing her former GNSR number 49. In reality, she was never previously painted

Former LNER design, Class K1 locomotive, number 62005, pictured at Leeds Holbeck Shed in late 1967, shortly before being withdrawn from service. (© PC)

Former LNER (GNSR) Class D40 locomotive, number 62277 *Gordon Highlander*, pictured in steam as a light engine at Aberdeen circa 1949. *(© PC)*

in GNSR Green livery, as when she entered service in 1920 she was painted black.

Number 62277 later moved to Dawsholm Shed in Glasgow, from where she worked special trains until 1966, when she was donated to the Glasgow Transport Museum. Her owners, the Glasgow Corporation, later loaned her to the Scottish Railway Museum on the Bo'ness and Kinneil Railway at Bo'ness, West Lothian in Scotland, to be put on display. She has remained on public display at the Museum ever since.

4-4-0 LNER (NB) Class D34 Locomotive, No. 62469 *Glen Douglas*

Number 62469 was built at the North British Railway, Cowlairs Works,

Glasgow, in September 1913 as an NBR K Class or Glen Class locomotive, number 256, *Glen Douglas*. These locomotives were built for mixed traffic use in Scotland but they were mainly used to work passenger trains on the West Highland Line. They also worked passenger services from Glasgow to Edinburgh via Polmont as well as passenger trains between Glasgow and Dundee. Number 62469 was later re-classified as an LNER Class D34 number 9256 and later LNER number 2469. She became BR 62469 in 1949.

During her BR service, 62469 worked out of engine sheds at Glasgow Eastfield (January 1948–May 1953), Aberdeen Kittybrewster (May 1953–February 1956) and Keith Shed in Moray (February 1956–November 1959).

Former LNER Class D34 locomotive, number 62469 *Glen Douglas*, pictured at an unknown location in Scotland during the late 1950s. *(© PC)*

She was officially withdrawn from BR service in November 1959.

After being withdrawn, 62469 was preserved and restored to her NBR Livery. She moved to Dawsholm Locomotive Shed in Glasgow where she was put back into BR service to work main line excursions and charter trains. She was finally withdrawn from BR service in 1962 and donated by the British Transport Commission to Glasgow Corporation to be put on display in the Glasgow Museum of Transport.

Number 62469 *Glen Douglas* remains on public display and can be seen in the Glasgow Museum of Transport, Riverside Museum, Pointhouse Quay, Glasgow, Scotland.

4-4-0 LNER (GCR) Class D11 Locomotive No. 62660 *Butler-Henderson*

Number 62660 was named after The Hon. Eric Brand Butler-Henderson, a former captain in the British Army who was later appointed the last new Director of the Great Central Railway before it was absorbed into the LNER in 1923. Butler-Henderson then became a Director of the LNER.

Number 62660 was built at the Gorton Locomotive Works, Manchester, in December 1919 as GCR Class 11F locomotive number 506. After the 1923 railway groupings, she was re-classified as LNER Class D11 number 5506 and later re-numbered LNER 2660. After 1948 she became BR number 62660.

Former LNER (GCR) Class D11 or Large Director Class locomotive, number 62660 (LNER 2660), *Butler-Henderson*, pictured at Doncaster in 1948. She is in a dilapidated condition but still painted in what remains of her LNER livery. *(© PC)*

She was originally built as an express passenger locomotive to work the GCR main line from London Marylebone to Manchester, via Rugby, Leicester, Nottingham and Sheffield. The line closed in 1966. During her later years, after coming under BR ownership, 62660 worked at Immingham, Manchester, Lincoln and finally Sheffield, from where she was withdrawn from service in November 1960.

Number 62660 was subsequently preserved as a part of the National Collection and put on public display at the BTC Museum in Clapham, London. In 1975, she was loaned to the GCR until 1992 when she returned home to the National Railway Museum in York, where she went on public display in the main hall.

Since 2009, 62660 has been on loan to the Barrow Hill Roundhouse where she is on public display.

2-4-0 LNER (GER) Class E4 Locomotive, No. 62785

Number 62785 was built at Stratford in January 1895 as GER Class T26 locomotive number 490. After the 1923 railway groupings, she was re-classified as an LNER Class E4 locomotive, number 7490. She later became LNER 7802, then LNER 2785 under a renumbering scheme. After 1948, she became BR number 62785.

A total of one hundred Class T26 (E4) locomotives were designed for working secondary passenger services but they quickly became successful as mixed traffic locomotives, earning themselves the nickname 'intermediates'. They worked the whole of the former GER network, performing a variety of duties. Withdrawals started in the 1920s but eighteen survived into the British Railways era and continued working until the mid-1950s when the introduction of diesel railcars effectively made them redundant. Number 62785 was the only Class E4 to survive beyond 1957. She was withdrawn from Cambridge on 31 December 1959.

Having been earmarked for preservation, 62785 subsequently became a part of the National Collection owned by the National Railway Museum in York. She is currently on loan to the Bressingham Steam Museum in Norfolk, where she can be seen on public display.

0-8-0 LNER (NER) Class Q6 Locomotive, No. 63395

Number 63395 was built at Darlington in December 1918 as NER Raven design Class T2 locomotive number 2238. After the 1923 railway groupings, 63395 was re-classified as an LNER Class Q6 number 3395, and after 1948 was renumbered BR 63395.

Former LNER Class E4 locomotive number 62785, pictured at Mildenhall Station in Suffolk in 1958, about to depart with a local two-coach passenger train service to Cambridge. The Cambridge to Mildenhall railway line closed to passenger traffic in 1962 and the line was completely closed in 1965. (© PC)

Former LNER Class Q6 locomotive, number 63395, pictured at Pontefract, West Yorkshire, on 29 December 1958 whilst working a goods train. *(© PC)*

Former LNER Class Q6 locomotive, number 63395, pictured at Pontefract Monkhill Station, working an up coal train in 1956. *(© PC)*

Former LNER Class Q6 locomotive, number 63395, pictured at Pontefract, West Yorkshire, on 22 May 1958 whilst working a down goods train between Sheffield and York. *(© PC)*

Former LNER Class Q6 locomotive, number 63395, pictured on 9 March 1957, hauling an empty coal train through Pontefract Baghill Station. *(© PC)*

Former LNER Class Q6 locomotive, number 63395, pictured working a coal train through Pontefract Monkhill Station on a cold winter's day during the winter of 1956/57. (© PC)

She was designed and built as a heavy freight locomotive and after entering service, spent a short period of time at Gateshead before being moved to Blaydon where she remained for twenty-five years. As part of a reshuffle during the Second World War, she was moved to Newport Shed, Middlesbrough. Number 63395 later worked out of various sheds in the north-east of England before being withdrawn from service whilst based at Sunderland South Dock in September 1967.

After being withdrawn from service, 63395 was stored at Tyne Dock Shed until she was purchased for preservation by the North Eastern Locomotive Preservation Group with a view to her being used on the North Yorkshire Moors Heritage

Railway. In June 1970, with restoration complete, 63395 was taken to Grosmont on the NYMR to start work. She has remained there ever since and her current boiler certificate is valid until 2024.

0-8-0 LNER (NER) Class Q7 Locomotive, No. 63460

Number 63460 was built at Darlington Works in October 1919 as Raven Class T3 number NER 901. After the 1923 railway groupings she was re-classified as an LNER Class Q7 and later allocated LNER number 3460. After 1948 she became BR 63460.

She started work at Blaydon but moved to Hull (Dairycoates) in 1923, to work heavy coal trains from the South

Yorkshire Coalfield to Hull Docks. She continued working in the north-east of England and her final years were spent at South Shields from where she worked heavy iron ore trains to Consett Steel Works, a job for which she was ideally suited. She was withdrawn from service in December 1962.

Number 63460 was subsequently preserved as a part of the National Collection owned by the National Railway Museum in York. She was moved to Darlington from where she made some local rail tours in the early 1960s, after which she visited London and Brighton. She returned to York in 1978 before being loaned to the North Eastern Locomotive Preservation Group.

She was later transported to Grosmont on the North Yorkshire Moors Railway where she underwent restoration and received an overhaul. She then worked on the NYM Railway from 1988 until 2004 when she was put on static display at the, then new, Railway Museum, Locomotion at Shildon. She is currently on public display at the Head of Steam Museum in Darlington and remains a part of the National Collection.

0-6-0 LNER (NER) Class J21 Locomotive, No. 65033

Number 65033 was built at Gateshead by the NER in March 1889 as a Class C two cylinder compound locomotive number NER 876. She was converted to a simple

Former LNER (NER) Class Q7 locomotive, number 63460, pictured as a light engine at Darlington Shed in the early 1950s. (© PC)

Former LNER (NER) Class J21 locomotive, number 65033, pictured as a light locomotive under steam at Darlington circa 1949. *(© PC)*

engine in 1908 when she was fitted with nineteen-inch cylinders and piston valves. After the railway groupings of 1923, NER 876 was re classified as LNER Class J21 number 876 and later allocated LNER number 5033. In December 1948 she became BR 65033.

She was initially withdrawn from service in November 1939, but due to the outbreak of war, her services were required, so repairs were carried out and she was put back into service. She then continued working for over twenty years in the north-east of England until she was finally withdrawn from service in April 1962.

After being withdrawn, 65033 was stored at Darlington to be preserved as a part of the National Collection, but it was later decided to remove her from the list of engines to be preserved. This was due to the fact that 65033 was no longer in the 'as built' condition due to her conversion from a compound engine to a simple engine, which had taken place in 1908.

After it was decided that number 65033 would no longer be preserved as a part of the National Collection, she remained at Darlington and arrangements were made for her to be scrapped. Fortunately, she was saved at the eleventh hour by the intervention of Mr Frank Atkinson, Director of the Beamish Museum in County Durham. Just four days before she was due to be towed away for scrap she was rescued and later restored at Tanfield before being transported to the nearby Beamish Museum

in 1972. She spent the next twelve years hauling wagons at the open air museum until her boiler certificate expired. She remained at Beamish until March 2009, when she was purchased by The Locomotive Conservation and Learning Trust with the aim of restoring her to work on the Stainmore Railway at Kirkby Stephen in Cumbria.

Number 65033 was later put on public display at the NRM at Shildon, before being transported to her new home at Kirkby Stephen in Cumbria. In October 2019, work commenced on stripping her down in readiness for a complete overhaul. After the overhaul is complete, number 65033 will be turned out in LNER green livery and put to work on the Stainmore Railway, hopefully for many years.

0-6-0 LNER (NBR) Class J36 Locomotive, No. 65243 *Maude*

Number 65243 was built by Neilson & Company at the Cowlairs Works (NBR), Glasgow, in December 1891. She entered service as NBR Class C locomotive number 673. In 1915 she was rebuilt with a larger boiler. After the 1923 groupings, she was re-classified as LNER, Class J36 number 9673, and later, LNER number 9643. She became BR 65243 after nationalisation took place in 1948.

Number 65243 spent the whole of her working life in Scotland apart from a two-year period from 1917 until 1919 when she was shipped to France to be used as a part of the war effort. Upon her return she was given the name *Maude* after Lt.

Former LNER (NER) Class J21 locomotive, number 65033, pictured at Barnard Castle, whilst working an RCTS rail tour from Darlington to Carlisle on 7 March 1960. (© PC)

Former LNER (NBR) Class J36 locomotive, number 65243 *Maude,* pictured at Bathgate Shed, West Lothian, Scotland, circa 1964. *(© PC)*

General Sir Frederick Stanley Maude, an eminent British Army officer at the time.

She was withdrawn from service at Bathgate, West Lothian, in July 1966, and in November that year she was purchased by the Scottish Railway Preservation Society. In 1980, 65243 successfully steamed from Scotland to Liverpool and back to take part in the 150th Anniversary of the Liverpool & Manchester Railway. She then worked a number of rail tours during the 1980s before returning home to work on the Bo'ness and Kinneil Railway in Scotland where she is still based.

0-6-0 LNER (NER) Class J27 Locomotive, No. 65894

Number 65894 was built at Darlington to an NER Class P3 design and entered service with the LNER on 30 September 1923.

She was re-classified as an LNER Class J27 and allocated LNER number 2392. She was initially assigned to Darlington Shed and later to Ferryhill in County Durham, where she worked local coal trains. In 1930, 65894 was transferred to York to work goods trains between York and Scarborough. In 1946 she was renumbered LNER 5894, and after 1948 she became BR number 65894.

After being taken into the BR locomotive stock, 65894 was removed from ordinary duties and assigned to the British Railways Civil Engineering Department at York to haul their departmental maintenance trains. In October 1966, 65894 moved to Sunderland South Dock Shed to work coal trains in east Durham and was the last locomotive at the shed when she was withdrawn from service on 30 September 1967, exactly forty-four years after being built.

Former LNER Class J27 locomotive, number 65894, pictured as a light engine on the turntable at Pontefract Baghill Station on 3 April 1958. *(© PC)*

Former LNER Class J27 locomotive, number 65894, pictured coupled to a track-laying ballast hopper in the Civil Engineering Department Yard at York in 1966. *(© PC)*

Former LNER locomotive, number 65894, pictured at Pontefract, West Yorkshire, in 1956. *(© PC)*

Former LNER locomotive, number 65894, pictured at York in 1965, fitted with a snow plough in preparation for snow clearing duties. *(© PC)*

Former LNER locomotive, number 65894, pictured at Pontefract, West Yorkshire, on 29 May 1956, hauling an empty engineers' permanent way maintenance train. *(© PC)*

In December 1967, 65894 was purchased by the North Eastern Railway Preservation Group, who fully restored her and transported her to a new home on the North Yorkshire Moors Railway. For almost fifty years, 65894 spent her time working on the NYMR but did on occasions visit other heritage railways. She can still be seen on the NYMR where she is fully operational.

0-4-0T LNER Class Y1 Tank Locomotive, No. 68153

Number 68153 was built by Sentinel (Shrewsbury) Ltd for the LNER and entered service on 31 December 1933 as LNER number 59. She later became LNER 8153 and BR 68153.

These Sentinel locomotives had a centre engine design based on the design of their steam lorries, which had vertical boilers and a chain drive to the wheels. They were specifically designed as shunting engines for use in railway depots and small yards. They were extremely economical on fuel and could be operated by one person. Their water-tube boilers meant that steam could be raised much more quickly than a locomotive with a conventional fire-tube boiler. These small engines were almost entirely used for shunting duties and seldom used for hauling trains due to their slow speed.

From 1948, number 68153 was assigned to work solely in the Geneva Permanent Way Yard at Darlington. In October 1954,

Former LNER Class Y1 Sentinel Tank locomotive, number 68153 (Railway Departmental Engine Number 54), pictured carrying out shunting duties at the Geneva Permanent Way Yard, Darlington, in the mid/late 1950s. *(© PC)*

she was re-numbered as a Permanent Way Departmental Stock locomotive number 54, the number being displayed on the cab-side as can be seen in the picture. She continued working for the department until being withdrawn from service on 30 June 1961. She was later purchased for preservation to work on the Middleton Private Railway in Leeds where she continues to operate.

CHAPTER 5

BR – BRITISH RAILWAYS LOCOMOTIVES

4-6-2 BR Britannia Class 7 Locomotive, No. 70000 *Britannia*

Number 70000 was built at Crewe in January 1951 and named *Britannia*, even though the name was already being used on Jubilee class locomotive number 45700. The Jubilee locomotive was re-named *Amethyst*.

Throughout the 1950s, 70000 was used to work express passenger boat trains from London (Liverpool Street) to Harwich to connect with ferry services to Holland. During the 1960s, she worked out of sheds at Willesden, Crewe and Manchester (Newton Heath), from where she was withdrawn from service in May 1966.

After being withdrawn, she was destined to be preserved as a part of the National Collection at York Railway Museum but that honour was eventually

BR locomotive number 70000 *Britannia* pictured at Doncaster Plant (Railway Works), on 20 September 1953, when it was open to members of the public to mark its centenary (1853–1953). The locomotive, which was less than three years old at the time, was a star attraction amongst the visitors. *(© PC)*

given to her sister locomotive, 70013 *Oliver Cromwell*, and 70000 was sold to a private concern. During the years that followed, 70000 worked on the Severn Valley Railway and the Nene Valley Railway as well as working special main line services. She went through changes of ownership but was constantly dogged by mechanical problems which necessitated costly repairs.

In 2009, 70000 was purchased by her current owner, The Royal Scot Locomotive & General Trust. After an extensive overhaul 70000 returned to service on the main line, and despite ongoing mechanical problems and prolonged absences from service for repairs and maintenance, she continues to serve enthusiasts and passengers by operating special excursions and rail tours from her home base at Crewe.

4-6-2 BR Britannia Class 7 Locomotive, No. 70013 *Oliver Cromwell*

Number 70013 was built at Crewe in May 1951 and assigned to Norwich Thorpe Shed. Throughout the 1950s, she could be seen working express passenger services between Norwich and London. In 1961 she was transferred to March Shed in Cambridgeshire before being moved to Carlisle in 1963, where she worked as a mixed traffic locomotive. Number 70013 was transferred to Carnforth in January 1968, and in August of that year she worked the Manchester to Carlisle leg of the 'Fifteen Guinea Special', it being the last official steam operated passenger train to work under BR on the railway network.

Number 70013 was subsequently preserved as a part of the national

British Railways Standard Class 7 (Britannia Class) locomotive, number 70013 *Oliver Cromwell*, pictured at Pontefract, West Yorkshire, hauling a Newcastle to Bournemouth express on 23 July 1960. *(© PC)*

collection but went on immediate loan to the Bressingham Steam Museum in Norfolk, where she remained for some thirty-six years before being taken to York in 2004. After the York 2004 Rail Festival, 70013 went on loan to the Great Central Railway at Loughborough where she was given a complete overhaul before working main line special excursion trains.

In 2019, number 70013 was taken out of service for a further overhaul, which commenced in March of that year. The NRM agreed that the locomotive could remain with the GCR until the end of 2021, at which time, a further loan agreement will be put in place which will include her operational duties in respect of main line running.

2-10-0 BR Standard Class 9F Locomotive, No. 92203
(Given the name *Black Prince* during preservation.)

Number 92203 was built at Swindon and entered service on 6 April 1959, when she was assigned to St Phillips Marsh Shed in Bristol. She later worked out of Old Oak Common Shed in West London before being moved to Banbury. Her work involved hauling heavy freight and mineral trains. In September 1966, she was assigned to Birkenhead in order to work iron ore trains from Bidston Dock at Birkenhead to Shotton Steel Works in Flintshire. She was withdrawn from service in November 1967 after working less than nine years.

After being withdrawn, 92203 was purchased directly from BR by the former artist and steam enthusiast, the late David Shepherd, and moved to the Longmoor Military Railway in Hampshire. Although un-named whilst in BR service, she was named by David Shepherd as *Black Prince*.

Number 92203 *Black Prince* was moved to the East Somerset Railway in 1973, and after visiting several other heritage railways, was taken to the Gloucestershire Warwickshire Steam Railway where

British Railways Standard Class 9F locomotive, number 92203, pictured at Grange Court Junction in Gloucestershire in August 1964 whilst hauling an iron-ore train. (*© PC*)

she received an overhaul in 2004. She worked there until 2011, when she moved to the North Norfolk Railway. After receiving a further overhaul, 92203 *Black Prince* re-entered service in 2014 and the following year she was purchased by the North Norfolk Railway. Number 92203 continued working on the NNR until March 2019, when she was taken out of service after cracks were discovered in the firebox shoulders. Repairs were carried out and she returned to service on the NNR in August 2019 where she continues to work.

2-10-0 BR Standard Class 9F Locomotive, No. 92220 *Evening Star*

Number 92220 *Evening Star* was built at Swindon and was the last steam locomotive ever built for BR. As a result, she was earmarked for preservation as part of the National Collection from the time she was built. A total of 251 BR Class 9F locomotives were built at Crewe and Swindon, numbered 92000 to 92250. Although 92220 *Evening Star* was the last locomotive of the class to be built,

she was not allocated the last sequential number. This was due to numbers being allocated to Crewe and Swindon in advance of the locomotives being built. The last locomotives built at the Crewe Works were allocated numbers from 92221 to 92250, before *Evening Star* was completed. When she entered service, *Evening Star* was allocated the last Swindon number, which was 92220. A total of nine Class 9F locomotives were subsequently preserved after being withdrawn from BR service. The remainder were scrapped.

Number 92220 entered service on 31 March 1960 painted in Brunswick Green livery with a copper capped chimney. All other members of the class were painted black. Despite being built for heavy freight duties, due to her special status, she spent almost all her BR service hauling passenger trains. She initially worked express passenger services between Cardiff and London Paddington before moving to the former Somerset and Dorset Railway to work passenger services

BR Standard Class 9F locomotive, number 92220 *Evening Star*, pictured working a passenger train on the former Somerset and Dorset Railway line at Templecombe in August 1963. *(© MC)*

BR Standard Class 9F locomotive, number 92220 *Evening Star*, pictured at Templecombe Lower Station on 19 August 1963, working a passenger train on the former Somerset and Dorset railway line from Bournemouth to Bath Green Park. The line closed in 1966 but Bath Green Park Station was given the status of a grade 2 listed building and preserved. (© MC)

BR 2-10-0, Standard Class 9F locomotive, number 92220 *Evening Star*, pictured at Cardiff General Station, about to depart with an express passenger train to London Paddington on 13 August 1960. (© PC)

BR 2-10-0, Standard Class 9F locomotive, number 92220 *Evening Star*, pictured at Templecombe Upper Station, working a Bath to Bournemouth passenger train on 19 August 1963. (© MC)

between Bath and Bournemouth. She was eventually withdrawn from service on 31 March 1965 after working for just five years with BR.

After being withdrawn from service in March 1965, 92220 was given an overhaul at Crewe before being put into storage at Brighton. In July 1973, she was loaned to the Keighley & Worth Valley Railway, where she worked, until moving to the newly opened National Railway Museum at Leeman Road, York, in March 1975.

Number 92220 later operated a number of main line specials and worked on the West Somerset Heritage Railway during their 1989 summer season. The following year (1990), 92220 was put on static display at Swindon Railway Museum whilst refurbishments were being carried out at the York Museum.

After the refurbishments had been completed, *Evening Star* returned home and has since been proudly on public display in the Main Hall at the National Railway Museum in York.

Number 92220 was the only member of her class to receive a name during BR service. This was selected from a list of suggested names which had been submitted by railway employees, following a competition which appeared in a British Railways (Western Region) Staff Magazine in 1959. A total of three employees were declared equal winners of the competition after each submitted the name *Evening Star*. The nameplates were affixed to the smoke deflectors on the locomotive, together with a commemorative plaque which appears beneath each nameplate. They can clearly be seen in the photographs.

CHAPTER 6

LIST OF PRESERVED STEAM LOCOMOTIVES

Great Western Railway Locomotives

* Denotes locomotives pictured in this book

NO	NAME/ OTHER INFO	WHEEL LAYOUT	CLASS	OWNER/LOCATION
426	(TVR No85)	0-6-2T	TVR 02	Keighley & Worth Valley Railway
450	(TVR No28)	0-6-2T	TVR 01	Dean Forest Railway
813	(PTR** No26)	0-6-0ST	PTR** (UC}	Severn Valley Railway
(** Above – denotes, Port Talbot Railway & Dock Company)				
1338	(Cardiff Railway No5)	0-4-0ST	UC	Didcot Railway Centre
1340	*Trojan*	0-4-0ST	UC	Didcot Railway Centre
1363		0-6-0ST	1361	Didcot Railway Centre
1369		0-6-0PT	1366	South Devon Railway
1420*		0-4-2T	1400	South Devon Railway
1442*		0-4-2T	1400	Tiverton Museum (Devon)
1450		0-4-2T	1400	Severn Valley Railway
1466		0-4-2T	1400	Didcot Railway Centre
1501		0-6-0PT	1500	Severn Valley Railway
1638		0-6-0PT	1600	Kent & East Sussex Railway
2516	(Dean Goods Locomotive)	0-6-0	2301	Swindon Railway Museum
2807*		2-8-0	2800	Gloucestershire Warwickshire Railway
2818		2-8-0	2800	Swindon Railway Museum
2857		2-8-0	2800	Severn Valley Railway
2859		2-8-0	2800	Llangollen Railway
2861		2-8-0	2800	Llangollen Railway
Locomotive 2861, above, was cut up in 2014 to supply donor parts for other restoration projects.				
2873		2-8-0	2800	South Devon Railway
Locomotive 2873, above, is partially dismantled, with parts having been removed and used in other restoration projects The future of the locomotive is uncertain but it is unlikely to steam again.				
2874*		2-8-0	2800	Gloucestershire Warwickshire Railway

NO	NAME/ OTHER INFO	WHEEL LAYOUT	CLASS	OWNER/LOCATION
2885		2-8-0	2884	Birmingham (Tyseley). Being restored
3205		0-6-0	2251	South Devon Railway
3440	*City of Truro*	4-4-0	3700 (City Class)	National Railway Museum
3650		0-6-0PT	5700	Didcot Railway Centre
3738		0-6-0PT	5700	Didcot Railway Centre
3802		2-8-0	2884	Llangollen Railway
3803		2-8-0	2884	South Devon Railway
3814		2-8-0	2884	North Yorkshire Moors Railway
3822		2-8-0	2884	Didcot Railway Centre
3845		2-8-0	2884	Dinmore Manor Locomotive Ltd

Number 3845, above, is still in scrapyard condition. Her boiler has been used to restore GWR No3850 and her remaining parts are destined to be used in other restoration projects. She is unlikely to be restored.

NO	NAME/ OTHER INFO	WHEEL LAYOUT	CLASS	OWNER/LOCATION
3850		2-8-0	2884	Owned by Dinmore Manor Loco Ltd

Normally works on the West Somerset Railway. Currently on the Glos Warwickshire Railway for overhaul.

NO	NAME/ OTHER INFO	WHEEL LAYOUT	CLASS	OWNER/LOCATION
3855		2-8-0	2884	East Lancashire Railway
4003	*Lode Star*	4-6-0	4000 (Star Class)	National Railway Museum
4073	*Caerphilly Castle*	4-6-0	4073 (Castle Class)	NRM (On display at Swindon)
4079*	*Pendennis Castle*	4-6-0	4073 (Castle Class)	Didcot Railway Centre
4110	(Large Prairie Tank)	2-6-2T	5101	West Somerset Railway
4115	(Large Prairie Tank)	2-6-2T	5101	Great Western Society

Number 4115, above, has donated parts for other restoration projects and is now unlikely to be restored.

NO	NAME/ OTHER INFO	WHEEL LAYOUT	CLASS	OWNER/LOCATION
4121	(Large Prairie Tank)	2-6-2T	5101	Birmingham (Tyseley)
4141	(Large Prairie Tank)	2-6-2T	5101	Epping Ongar Railway
4144*	(Large Prairie Tank)	2-6-2T	5101	Didcot Railway Centre
4150	(Large Prairie Tank)	2-6-2T	5101	Severn Valley Railway
4160*	(Large Prairie Tank)	2-6-2T	5101	West Somerset Railway
4247		2-8-0T	4200	Bodmin & Wenford Railway
4248		2-8-0T	4200	Swindon Railway Museum
4253		2-8-0T	4200	Kent & East Sussex Railway
4270		2-8-0T	4200	Gloucestershire Warwickshire Railway
4277		2-8-0T	4200	Dartmouth Steam Railway
4555*	*Warrior*	2-6-2T	4500	Dartmouth Steam Railway

Number 4555 (above) is a Small Prairie Tank locomotive, given the name *Warrior* whilst in preservation.

NO	NAME/ OTHER INFO	WHEEL LAYOUT	CLASS	OWNER/LOCATION
4561	(Small Prairie Tank)	2-6-2T	4500	West Somerset Railway
4566	(Small Prairie Tank)	2-6-2T	4500	Severn Valley Railway
4588	*Trojan*	2-6-2T	4575	Peak Railway (Derbyshire)

Number 4588 (above), was given the name *Trojan* whilst in preservation.

NO	NAME/ OTHER INFO	WHEEL LAYOUT	CLASS	OWNER/LOCATION
4612		0-6-0PT	5700	Bodmin and Wenford Railway
4920	*Dumbleton Hall*	4-6-0	4900 (Hall Class)	South Devon Railway
4930*	*Hagley Hall*	4-6-0	4900 (Hall Class)	Severn Valley Railway
4936*	*Kinlet Hall*	4-6-0	4900 (Hall Class)	South Devon Railway
4942	*Maindy Hall*	4-6-0	4900 (Hall Class)	Didcot Railway Centre
Number 4942 (above), is being converted to a new Saint Class locomotive No. 2999 *Lady of Legend.*				
4953*	*Pitchford Hall*	4-6-0	4900 (Hall Class)	Epping Ongar Railway
4965	*Rood Ashton Hall*	4-6-0	4900 (Hall Class)	Birmingham (Tyseley)
4979*	*Wootton Hall*	4-6-0	4900 (Hall Class)	Ribble Steam Railway
5029*	*Nunney Castle*	4-6-0	4073 (Castle Class)	Crewe (Owner Jeremy Hosking)
5043*	*Earl of Mount Edgcumbe*	4-6-0	4073 (Castle Class)	Birmingham (Tyseley)
5051*	*Earl Bathurst*	4-6-0	4073 (Castle Class)	Didcot Railway Centre
When built in May 1936, locomotive number 5051 (above), was given the name *Dryslkyn Castle*. She was renamed *Earl Bathurst* in 1937. Both names have been used at different times during preservation.				
5080	*Defiant*	4-6-0	4073 (Castle Class)	Birmingham (Tyseley)
Number 5080 (above), was named *Ogmore Castle* when built in 1939. Renamed *Defiant* in 1941.				
5164	(Large Prairie Tank)	2-6-2T	5101	Severn Valley Railway
5193*	(Large Prairie Tank)	2-6-2T	5101	West Somerset Railway
Number 5193 (above), has been converted into a GWR, 2-6-0, 9300 Class locomotive (since being preserved) and now operates as number 9351.				
5199	(Large Prairie Tank)	2-6-2T	5101	Llangollen Railway
5224		2-8-0T	5205	Peak Railway (Derbyshire)
5227		2-8-0T	5205	Didcot Railway Centre
Number 5227 (above) has been used to supply donor parts to other restoration projects. The axle boxes are being fitted to 4700 Class number 4709 and the boiler is destined to be used in the building of a County Class locomotive, number 3840, *County of Montgomery.*				
5239	*Goliath*	2-8-0T	5205	Dartmouth Steam Railway
Number 5239 (above) named after being preserved.				
5322		2-6-0	4300	Didcot Railway Centre
5521		2-6-2T	4575	Four Mill, Lydney (Dean Forest Railway)
5526		2-6-2T	4575	South Devon Railway
5532		2-6-2T	4575	Llangollen Railway
5538*		2-6-2T	4575	Dean Forest Railway
5539		2-6-2T	4575	Barry Island Railway (South Wales)

NO	NAME/ OTHER INFO	WHEEL LAYOUT	CLASS	OWNER/LOCATION
5541		2-6-2T	4575	Dean Forest Railway
5542		2-6-2T	4575	South Devon Railway
5552		2-6-2T	4575	Bodmin and Wenford Railway
5553*		2-6-2T	4575	Peak Railway (Derbyshire)
5572		2-6-2T	4575	Didcot Railway Centre
5619	(Owner: Telford Steam Railway)	0-6-2T	5600	Nene Valley Railway (On loan)
5637		0-6-2T	5600	East Somerset Railway
5643		0-6-2T	5600	Embsay & Bolton Abbey Steam Railway
5668		0-6-2T	5600	Kent & East Sussex Railway
5764		0-6-0PT	5700	Severn Valley Railway
5775	(Owner, KWVR)	0-6-0PT	5700	Loaned to the NRM, York
5786		0-6-0PT	5700	South Devon Railway
5900	*Hinderton Hall*	4-6-0	4900 (Hall Class)	Didcot Railway Centre
5952	*Cogan Hall*	4-6-0	4900 (Hall Class)	Llangollen Railway
5967	*Bickmarsh Hall*	4-6-0	4900 (Hall Class)	Northampton & Lamport Railway
5972*	*Olton Hall / Hogwarts Castle*	4-6-0	4900 (Hall Class)	Harry Potter Museum, Watford
5972 (above) used in the Harry Potter films painted Crimson Red & bearing the name *Hogwarts Castle*.				
6000*	*King George V*	4-6-0	6000 (King Class)	National Railway Museum, York
6023	*King Edward II*	4-6-0	6000 (King Class)	Didcot Railway Centre
6024	*King Edward I*	4-6-0	6000 (King Class)	West Somerset Railway
6106		2-6-2T	6100	Didcot Railway Centre
6412		0-6-0PT	6400	South Devon Railway
6430		0-6-0PT	6400	Llangollen Railway
6435		0-6-0PT	6400	Bodmin & Wenford Railway
6619		0-6-2T	5600	Kent & East Sussex Railway
6634		0-6-2T	5600	Peak Railway Derbyshire
6686	(Still in scrapyard condition)	0-6-2T	5600	Barry Island Railway
6695		0-6-2T	5600	West Somerset Railway
6697*		0-6-2T	5600	Didcot Railway Centre
6960	*Raveningham Hall*	4-6-0	6959 (Modified Hall Class)	West Somerset Railway
6984	*Owsden Hall*	4-6-0	6959 (Mod Hall Class)	Swindon & Cricklade Railway
6989*	*Wightwick Hall*	4-6-0	6959 (Mod Hall Class)	Buckinghamshire Railway Centre

NO	NAME/ OTHER INFO	WHEEL LAYOUT	CLASS	OWNER/LOCATION
6990	*Witherslack Hall*	4-6-0	6959 (Mod Hall Class)	Great Central Railway
6998	*Burton Agnes Hall*	4-6-0	6959 (Mod Hall Class)	Didcot Railway Centre
7027	*Thornbury Castle*	4-6-0	4073 (Castle Class)	West Somerset Railway
7029*	*Clun Castle*	4-6-0	4073 (Castle Class)	Birmingham (Tyseley)
7200		2-8-2T	7200	Buckinghamshire Railway Centre
7202		2-8-2T	7200	Didcot Railway Centre
7229*		2-8-2T	7200	East Lancashire Railway
7325	(Ex-number 9303 – Pre 1958)	2-6-0	4300	Severn Valley Railway
7714		0-6-0PT	5700	Severn Valley Railway
7715	(Later sold to LT as number L 99)	0-6-0PT	5700	Bucks Railway Centre
7752		0-6-0PT	5700	Birmingham (Tyseley)
7754	(Owned by Nat Museum of Wales)	0-6-0PT	5700	Llangollen Railway
7760		0-6-0PT	5700	Birmingham (Tyseley)
7802	*Bradley Manor*	4-6-0	7800 (Manor Class)	Severn Valley Railway
7808	*Cookham Manor*	4-6-0	7800 (Manor Class)	Didcot Railway Centre
7812	*Erlestoke Manor*	4-6-0	7800 (Manor Class)	Severn Valley Railway
7819*	*Hinton Manor*	4-6-0	7800 (Manor Class)	Swindon (McArthur Glen)
7820*	*Dinmore Manor*	4-6-0	7800 (Manor Class)	Glos Warwickshire Rly
7821	*Ditcheat Manor*	4-6-0	7800 (Manor Class)	West Somerset Railway
7822	*Foxcote Manor*	4-6-0	7800 (Manor Class)	Llangollen Railway
7827	*Lydham Manor*	4-6-0	7800 (Manor Class)	Dartmouth Steam Railway
7828*	*Odney Manor*	4-6-0	7800 (Manor Class)	West Somerset Railway
7903	*Foremarke Hall*	4-6-0	6959 (Mod Hall Class)	Glos Warwickshire Rly
7927	*Willington Hall*	4-6-0	6959 (Mod Hall Class)	Llangollen Railway
Number 7927 (above) broken up for donor parts. Boiler destined for new build locomotive number 6880 *Betton Grange* and frames used for new build GWR number 1014, *County of Glamorgan*.				
9017	*Earl of Berkeley*	4-4-0	9000 (Dukedog or Earl Class)	Bluebell Railway

NO	NAME/ OTHER INFO	WHEEL LAYOUT	CLASS	OWNER/LOCATION
9400	(Owned by NRM)	0-6-0PT	9400	Swindon Railway Museum
9351*		2-6-0	9300	West Somerset Railway
9351 (above) was originally GWR, 2-6-2, Class 5101 Tank locomotive number 5193. She was subsequently converted to a 2-6-0 tender locomotive after being purchased for preservation.				
9466*		0-6-0PT	9400	Birmingham (Tyseley)
9600		0-6-0PT	5700	Birmingham (Tyseley)
9629		0-6-0PT	5700	Pontypool and Blaenavon Railway
9642		0-6-0PT	5700	Glos Warwickshire Railway
9681		0-6-0PT	5700	Dean Forest Railway
9682		0-6-0PT	5700	GWR Preservation Group, Southall

Southern Railway Locomotives

* Denotes locomotives pictured in this book

NO	NAME/ OTHER INFO	WHEEL LAYOUT	CLASS	OWNER/LOCATION
W24 *	*Calbourne*	0-4-4T	02	Isle of Wight Railway
30053		0-4-4T	M7	Swanage Railway
30064*		0-6-0T	USA	Bluebell Railway
30065	*Maunsell*	0-6-0T	USA	Kent & East Sussex Railway
30070	*Wainwright*	0-6-0T	USA	Kent & East Sussex Railway
30072		0-6-0T	USA	Keighley & Worth Valley Railway
30075		0-6-0T	USA	North Dorset Railway, Shillingstone
30076		0-6-0T	USA	North Dorset Railway, Shillingstone
30096	*Normandy*	0-4-0T	B4	Bluebell Railway
30102	*Granville*	0-4-0T	B4	Bressingham Steam Museum
30120*	(Owned by NRM)	4-4-0	T9	Bodmin & Wenford Railway
30245	(Owned by NRM)	0-4-4T	M7	National Railway Museum, York
30499		4-6-0	S15	Mid Hants Railway
30506		4-6-0	S15	Mid Hants Railway
30541*		0-6-0	Q	Bluebell Railway,
30583*		4-4-2T	0415	Bluebell Railway
30585*		2-4-0WT	0298	Buckinghamshire Railway Centre
30587		2-4-0WT	0298	NRM Shildon
30777	*Sir Lamiel* (Owned by NRM)	4-6-0	N15	Great Central Railway
30825		4-6-0	S15	North Yorkshire Moors Railway
30828	*Harry A. Frith*	4-6-0	S15	Mid Hants Railway
30830*		4-6-0	S15	North Yorkshire Moors Railway
30847		4-6-0	S15	Bluebell Railway

NO	NAME/ OTHER INFO	WHEEL LAYOUT	CLASS	OWNER/LOCATION
30850*	*Lord Nelson* (Owned by NRM)	4-6-0	LN (Lord Nelson Class)	Mid Hants Railway
30925*	*Cheltenham* (Owned by NRM)	4-4-0	V (Schools Class)	Mid Hants Railway
30926	*Repton*	4-4-0	V (Schools Class)	North Yorkshire Moors Railway
30928	*Stowe*	4-4-0	V (Schools Class)	Bluebell Railway
31027		0-6-0T	P	Bluebell Railway
31065*		0-6-0	01	Bluebell Railway
31178		0-6-0T	P	Bluebell Railway
31263		0-4-4T	H	Bluebell Railway
31323		0-6-0T	P	Bluebell Railway
31556		0-6-0T	P	Kent & East Sussex Railway
31592		0-6-0	C	Bluebell Railway
31618		2-6-0	U	Bluebell Railway
31625		2-6-0	U	Swanage Railway
31638		2-6-0	U	Bluebell Railway
31737 (No737)	(Owned by NRM)	4-4-0	D	National Railway Museum, York
31806		2-6-0	U	Swanage Railway
31874		2-6-0	N	Swanage Railway
32110	*Cannock Wood & Yarmouth*	0-6-0T	E1	Isle of Wight Steam Railway

Number 32110 (above) never carried that number whilst in service. She was built by the LBSCR as number 110 and later became SR number 2110. In 1927 the locomotive was sold to the Cannock & Rugeley Colliery Company where she was given the name and number, *Cannock Wood*, number 9. She was withdrawn from service in 1963 and subsequently preserved. She is currently owned by the IOW Steam Railway as number W2 *Yarmouth*.

NO	NAME/ OTHER INFO	WHEEL LAYOUT	CLASS	OWNER/LOCATION
32473 (No 473)	*Birch Grove*	0-6-2T	E4	Bluebell Railway
32636	*Fenchurch*	0-6-0T	A1X	Bluebell Railway
32640 (IOW No W11)	*Newport*	0-6-0T	A1X	Isle of Wight Steam Railway
32646* (IOW No W8)	*Freshwater*	0-6-0T	A1X	Isle of Wight Steam Railway

32646 above, was also named *Newington* whilst owned by the LBSCR from 1876 until 1903.

NO	NAME/ OTHER INFO	WHEEL LAYOUT	CLASS	OWNER/LOCATION
32650	*Whitechapel*	0-6-0T	A1X	Spa Valley Railway
32655*	*Stepney*	0-6-0T	A1X	Bluebell Railway
32662*	*Martello*	0-6-0T	A1X	Bressingham Steam Museum
32670	*Poplar*	0-6-0T	A1X	Kent & East Sussex Railway
32678	*Knowle*	0-6-0T	A1X	Kent & East Sussex Railway
33001*	(Owned by NRM)	0-6-0	Q1	National Railway Museum, York
34007	*Wadebridge*	4-6-2	WC	Mid Hants Railway
34010*	*Sidmouth*	4-6-2	WC	Swanage Railway
34016	*Bodmin*	4-6-2	WC	Carnforth for main line restoration
34023*	*Blackmore Vale*	4-6-2	WC	Bluebell Railway

NO	NAME/ OTHER INFO	WHEEL LAYOUT	CLASS	OWNER/LOCATION
34027*	*Taw Valley*	4-6-2	WC	Severn Valley Railway
34028*	*Eddystone*	4-6-2	WC	Swanage Railway
34039	*Boscastle*	4-6-2	WC	Great Central Railway
34046	*Braunton*	4-6-2	WC	Crewe for main line restoration
34051*	*Winston Churchill* (Owned by NRM)	4-6-2	BB	NRM, York (On display at Shildon)
34053	*Sir Keith Park*	4-6-2	BB	Swanage Railway
34058	*Sir Frederick Pile*	4-6-2	BB	Mid Hants Railway
34059*	*Sir Archibald Sinclair*	4-6-2	BB	Bluebell Railway
34067*	*Tangmere*	4-6-2	BB	Carnforth (West Coast Railways)
34070	*Manston*	4-6-2	BB	Swanage Railway
34072*	*257 Squadron*	4-6-2	BB	Swanage Railway
34073	*249 Squadron*	4-6-2	BB	Carnforth (West Coast Railways)
34081	*92 Squadron*	4-6-2	BB	Nene Valley Railway
34092*	*Wells / City of Wells*	4-6-2	WC	East Lancashire Railway
34101*	*Hartland*	4-6-2	WC	North Yorkshire Moors Railway
34105	*Swanage*	4-6-2	WC	Mid Hants Railway
35005*	*Canadian Pacific*	4-6-2	MN	Mid Hants Railway
35006*	*P & OSN Co*	4-6-2	MN	Glos Warwickshire Railway

Full name of number 35006 (above) is *Peninsular & Oriental Steam Navigation Company*. It is the longest name of any preserved steam locomotive.

NO	NAME/ OTHER INFO	WHEEL LAYOUT	CLASS	OWNER/LOCATION
35009	*Shaw Savill*	4-6-2	MN	Riley & Son (East Lancs Railway)
35010	*Blue Star*	4-6-2	MN	Colne Valley Railway
35011	*General Steam Navigation*	4-6-2	MN	Sellindge, Kent (for restoration)
35018	*British India Line*	4-6-2	MN	Carnforth (West Coast Railways)
35022*	*Holland-America Line*	4-6-2	MN	Crewe (LNWR Heritage)
35025	*Brocklebank Line*	4-6-2	MN	Sellindge, Kent (under restoration)
35027	*Port Line*	4-6-2	MN	Riley & Son (East Lancs Railway)
35028	*Clan Line*	4-6-2	MN	MN Loco Preservation Society, Southall
35029	*Ellerman Lines* (Owned by NRM)	4-6-2	MN	National Railway Museum, York
380S (SR) Ex-LBSCR No 82 (682)	*Boxhill*	0-6-0T	A1	National Railway Museum, York
LBSCR No 214 (later No 618)	*Gladstone*	0-4-2	B1	National Railway Museum, York
LSWR & SR No 563	(Donated by NRM, York)	4-4-0	T3	Swanage Railway

London Midland & Scottish Railway Locomotives

* Denotes locomotives pictured in this book

NO	NAME/ OTHER INFO	WHEEL LAYOUT	CLASS	OWNER/LOCATION
LNWR 1719	*Cornwall* (Owned by NRM)	4-2-2 (rebuilt 2-2-2)	UC	National Railway Museum, York
LMS 17916	(Highland Railway No 103)	4-6-0	4F	Glasgow Transport Museum
LMS 14010	(Caledonian Railway No 123)	4-2-2	1P	Glasgow Transport Museum
LMS 673	(Midland Railway 118 & 673)	4-2-2	MR Class 115	Displayed at NRM, York (Owners)
LMS 2271	(North Staffs Railway No 2)	0-6-2T	L	Foxfield Railway, Staffordshire
41000 (MR No 1000)	(Owned by NRM)	4-4-0	4P	Displayed at Barrow Hill Roundhouse
41241		2-6-2T	2MT	Keighley & Worth Valley Railway
41298*		2-6-2T	2MT	Isle of Wight Steam Railway
41312		2-6-2T	2MT	Mid Hants Railway
41313		2-6-2T	2MT	Isle of Wight Steam Railway
41708	(owner: Barrow Hill Engine Shed Soc)	0-6-0T	1F	Barrow Hill Roundhouse (display)
41966	*Thundersley* (Owned by NRM)	4-4-2T	3P	Bressingham Steam Museum (on loan)
42073*		2-6-4T	4MT	Lakeside & Haverthwaite Railway
42085		2-6-4T	4MT	Lakeside & Haverthwaite Railway
42500*	(Owned by NRM)	2-6-4T	4MT	National Railway Museum, York
42700*	(Owned by NRM)	2-6-0	5MT	National Railway Museum, York
42765		2-6-0	5MT	East Lancashire Railway
42859	(Dismantled – future uncertain)	2-6-0	5MT	Unknown location, Lincolnshire
42968		2-6-0	5MT	Severn Valley Railway
43106		2-6-0	4MT	Severn Valley Railway
43924		0-6-0	4F	Keighley & Worth Valley Railway
44027	(Owned by NRM)	0-6-0	4F	Glos Warwickshire Railway
44123		0-6-0	4F	Avon Valley Railway
44422*		0-6-0	4F	West Somerset Railway
44767*	*George Stephenson* (named in 1975)	4-6-0	5MT	North Norfolk Railway
44806	*Magpie*	4-6-0	5MT	NYMR
Number 44806 (above) was named *Magpie* in 1973 after being adopted by ITV children's series, Magpie.				
44871	*Sovereign*	4-6-0	5MT	East Lancashire Railway
Number 44871 (above) carried the name *Sovereign* in the late 1970s, whilst in preservation.				
44901		4-6-0	5MT	Glos Warwickshire Railway

NO	NAME/ OTHER INFO	WHEEL LAYOUT	CLASS	OWNER/LOCATION
44932		4-6-0	5MT	Usually operates main line services from the West Coast Railway's bases at Southall (West London) and Carnforth (Lancashire)
45000	(Owned by NRM)	4-6-0	5MT	NRM (On display at Shildon)
45025		4-6-0	5MT	Strathspey Railway
45110	*RAF Biggin Hill* (named in 1971)	4-6-0	5MT	Severn Valley Railway
45163		4-6-0	5MT	Colne Valley Railway
45212		4-6-0	5MT	Keighley & Worth Valley Railway
45231	(Owner: West Coast Railways)	4-6-0	5MT	Crewe (may move to Southall)
45293*		4-6-0	5MT	Colne Valley Railway
45305		4-6-0	5MT	Great Central Railway
45337		4-6-0	5MT	Llangollen Railway
45379		4-6-0	5MT	Mid Hants Railway
45407	*Lancashire Fusilier*	4-6-0	5MT	East Lancashire Railway
45428*	*Eric Treacy*	4-6-0	5MT	North Yorkshire Moors Railway
Number 45428 (above) named after being preserved.				
45491		4-6-0	5MT	Great Central Railway
45593*	*Kolhapur*	4-6-0	6P5F Jubilee	Birmingham (Tyseley)
45596*	*Bahamas*	4-6-0	6P5F Jubilee	Keighley & Worth Valley Railway
45690*	*Leander*	4-6-0	6P5F Jubilee	Carnforth (West Coast Railways)
45699*	*Galatea*	4-6-0	6P5F Jubilee	Carnforth (West Coast Railways)
46100*	*Royal Scot*	4-6-0	7P	Crewe Heritage Centre
46115*	*Scots Guardsman*	4-6-0	7P	Carnforth (West Coast Railways)
46201	*Princess Elizabeth*	4-6-2	8P	Midland Railway (Butterley)
46203	*Princess Margaret Rose*	4-6-2	8P	Midland Railway (Butterley)
46229	*Duchess of Hamilton*	4-6-2	8P	National Railway Museum, York
46233	*Duchess of Sutherland*	4-6-2	8P	Midland Railway (Butterley)
46235*	*City of Birmingham* (Owned by NRM)	4-6-2	8P	Birmingham Science Museum
46428		2-6-0	2MT	East Lancashire Railway
46441		2-6-0	2MT	Lakeside & Haverthwaite Railway
46443*		2-6-0	2MT	Severn Valley Railway
46447		2-6-0	2MT	East Somerset Railway
46464		2-6-0	2MT	Caledonian Railway
46512*		2-6-0	2MT	Strathspey Railway
46521		2-6-0	2MT	Great Central Railway
47279		0-6-0T	3F	Keighley & Worth Valley Railway

NO	NAME/ OTHER INFO	WHEEL LAYOUT	CLASS	OWNER/LOCATION
47298		0-6-0T	3F	East Lancashire Railway
47324		0-6-0T	3F	East Lancashire Railway
47327		0-6-0T	3F	Midland Railway (Butterley)
47357		0-6-0T	3F	Midland Railway (Butterley)
47383		0-6-0T	3F	Severn Valley Railway
47406*		0-6-0T	3F	Great Central Railway
47445		0-6-0T	3F	Midland Railway (Butterley)
47493		0-6-0T	3F	Spa Valley Railway
47564		0-6-0T	3F	Midland Railway (Butterley)
48151		2-8-0	8F	Carnforth (West Coast Railways)
48173		2-8-0	8F	Churnet Valley Railway
LMS 8274	(Ex-WD No. 70348)	2-8-0	8F	Great Central Railway

Although LMS number 8274 (above) was allocated to this engine in 1940, she never carried it and was renumbered WD 70348 shortly afterwards. In 1942, a locomotive built by the North British Company was allocated LMS number 8274 (later BR 48274), which she carried until withdrawn from service in September 1966. The locomotive was cut up a few months later.

NO	NAME/ OTHER INFO	WHEEL LAYOUT	CLASS	OWNER/LOCATION
48305		2-8-0	8F	Great Central Railway
48431		2-8-0	8F	Keighley & Worth Valley Railway
48518		2-8-0	8F	Keighley & Worth Valley Railway
48624		2-8-0	8F	Great Central Railway
48773		2-8-0	8F	Severn Valley Railway
49395	(Owned by NRM)	0-8-0	7F	NRM York (On display at Shildon)
50621	LYR No1008 (Owned by NRM)	2-4-2T	7F	National Railway Museum, York
51218	(LYR Class 21 Pug Engine)	0-4-0ST	0F	Keighley & Worth Valley Railway
52044	(LYR Class 25)	0-6-0	2F	Keighley & Worth Valley Railway
52322	(LYR Class 27)	0-6-0	3F	East Lancashire Railway
53808*	S&DJR	2-8-0	7F	West Somerset Railway
53809	S&DJR	2-8-0	7F	North Norfolk Railway
55189	Caledonian Railway	0-4-4T	2P	Bo'ness & Kinneil Railway
57566	Caledonian Class 812	0-6-0	3F	Strathspey Railway
58850*		0-6-0T	2F	Bluebell Railway
58926*	(Owned by National Trust)	0-6-2T	2F	Keighley & Worth Valley Railway
LMS 11243	(LYR Class 21, No 19)	0-4-0ST	0F	Ribble Steam Railway
LMS 11456	(LYR Class 23, No752)	0-6-0SR	2F	Keighley & Worth Valley Railway
LMS 14010	(Caledonian No123 + 1123)	4-2-2	1P	Glasgow Museum of Transport
LMS 17916	(Highland Railway No 103)	4-6-0	4F	Glasgow Museum of Transport
LMS 20002	(Midland No158, & No 2)	2-4-0	156 Class (MR)	National Railway Museum, York
LMS & Midland Railway No 673		4-2-2	115 Class (MR)	National Railway Museum, York

NO	NAME/ OTHER INFO	WHEEL LAYOUT	CLASS	OWNER/LOCATION
Grand Junction Railway No49	*Columbine*	2-2-2	UC	London Science Museum (Owned by NRM)
Furness Railway No3	*Coppernob*	0-4-0	A2	National Railway Museum, York
Furness Railway Numbers 20 & 25		0-4-0ST	UC	Owned by the Furness Railway Trust
Liverpool & Manchester Rly No 57	*Lion*	0-4-2	UC	On display at the Liverpool Museum
Mersey Railway No 5	*Cecil Raikes*	0-6-4T	UC	Liverpool Museum in storage (not displayed)

London & North Eastern Railway Locomotives

*Denotes locomotives pictured in this book

NO	NAME/ OTHER INFO	WHEEL LAYOUT	CLASS	OWNER/LOCATION
60007*	*Sir Nigel Gresley*	4-6-2	A4	North Yorkshire Moors Railway
60008*	*Dwight D. Eisenhower*	4-6-2	A4	National Railway Museum, Wisconsin, USA
60009*	*Union of South Africa*	4-6-2	A4	Owned by John Cameron, Fife, Scotland
60010*	*Dominion of Canada*	4-6-2	A4	Canadian Railway Museum, Quebec, Canada
60019*	*Bittern*	4-6-2	A4	Owned by Jeremy Hosking Based at Crewe
60022*	*Mallard* (Owned by NRM)	4-6-2	A4	National Railway Museum, York (Displayed)
60103*	*Flying Scotsman* (Owned by NRM)	4-6-2	A3	Tours the UK. Based at the NRM, York
60532	*Blue Peter*	4-6-2	A2	Owned by Jeremy Hosking. Based at Crewe
60800	*Green Arrow* (Owned by NRM)	2-6-2	V2	NRM, York (On display at Shildon)
61264		4-6-0	B1	North Yorkshire Moors Railway
61306*	*Mayflower*	4-6-0	B1	Owned by David Buck
Number 61306 (above) was an unnamed locomotive until the name *Mayflower* was given to her during preservation. The name was originally used on Class B1 locomotive 61379 which was scrapped in 1962.				
61572	(Owned by the Midland & GN Society)	4-6-0	B12	North Norfolk Railway
61994	*Great Marquess*	2-6-0	K4	Bo'ness & Kinneil Railway
62005*		2-6-0	K1	North Yorkshire Moors Railway

NO	NAME/ OTHER INFO	WHEEL LAYOUT	CLASS	OWNER/LOCATION
62277*	*Gordon Highlander*	4-4-0	D40	Glasgow Transport Museum
Number 62277 (above) is currently on loan to the Bo'ness & Kinneil Railway Museum where she is on display.				
62469*	*Glen Douglas*	4-4-0	D34	Glasgow Transport Museum
62660*	*Butler-Henderson* (Owned by NRM)	4-4-0	D11	Derby Roundhouse (Displayed)
62712	*Morayshire*	4-4-0	D49	Bo'ness & Kinneil Railway
62785*	(Owned by NRM)	2-4-0	E4	On loan to Bressingham Museum
63395*		0-8-0	Q6	North Yorkshire Moors Railway
63460*	(Owned by NRM)	0-8-0	Q7	Shildon Locomotion Museum
63601	(Built as GCR Class 8K) (Owned by NRM)	2-8-0	O4	Great Central Railway (on loan)
65033*		0-6-0	J21	Stainmore Railway (Kirkby Stephen)
65243*	*Maude*	0-6-0	J36	Bo'ness & Kinneil Railway
65462		0-6-0	J15	North Norfolk Railway
65567	(Owned by NRM)	0-6-0	J17	Barrow Hill Roundhouse Derbyshire
65894*	(Owned by NE Loco Pres Group)	0-6-0	J27	Darlington Railway Museum
68077	(LNER 8077) (WD 71466)	0-6-0ST	J94	Spa Valley Railway
68078	(LNER 8078) (WD 71463)	0-6-0ST	J94	Hope Farm, Sellindge, Kent
68088	(LNER 985)	0-4-0T	Y7	North Norfolk Railway
68095		0-4-0ST	Y9	Bo'ness & Kinneil Railway
68153*	(LNER, Dept No54)	0-4-0T	Y1	Middleton Railway, Leeds
68633	(Owned by NRM)	0-6-0T	J69	Bressingham Steam Museum (On loan)
68846	(Owned by NRM)	0-6-0ST	J52	National Railway Museum, York
69023		0-6-0T	J72	Wensleydale Railway
69523		0-6-2T	N2	North Norfolk Railway
69621		0-6-2T	N7	Colchester Railway Museum
NER Number 1310		0-4-0T	Y7	Middleton Railway, Leeds
GNR 251	(LNER 251, 3251 & 2800)	4-4-2	C1	Owned by NRM. On display at Shildon
GNR 990	*Henry Oakley* (LNER 3990)	4-4-2	C2	National Railway Museum, York
LNER Number 66	*Aerolite*	2-2-4T	X1	National Railway Museum, York

NO	NAME/ OTHER INFO	WHEEL LAYOUT	CLASS	OWNER/LOCATION
GNR Number 1	(Stirling Single)	4-2-2	UC	Owned by NRM, York. On display at Shildon
NER Number 1463	(Tennant design)	2-4-0	E5	Owned by NRM, York. On display at Darlington
NER Number 910	(Owned by NRM)	2-4-0	901	Stainmore Railway, Kirkby Stephen
NER Number 1621	(Owned by NRM)	4-4-0	D17	Owned by NRM, York. On display at Shildon
NER Number 1275	(Owned by NRM)	0-6-0	1001	National Railway Museum, York (On display)
WD Number 196	(Built 1953 for the WD)	0-6-0ST	UC	'Stoomcentrum' Steam Railway, Belgium

WD No. 196 worked the Longmoor Military Railway, Hampshire, until 1966, when she was withdrawn from service. She was restored and given the identity of a former BR (LNER) Class J94 sister locomotive, number 68011, (LNER 8011), (WD 75119), to authenticate the use of LNER and BR livery during her preservation. The original locomotive 68011, which had been built in 1945, was scrapped in 1965. WD 196 was later named *Errol Lonsdale* before being sold to the Stoomcentrum Steam Railway where she continues to work. She is currently painted in BR black livery and displaying BR number 68011, which was originally carried by her sister locomotive.

British Railway Standard Class Locomotives

*Denotes locomotives pictured in this book

NO	NAME/ OTHER INFO	WHEEL LAYOUT	CLASS	OWNER/LOCATION
70000*	*Britannia*	4-6-2	7P6F	Royal Scot Trust based at Crewe
70013*	*Oliver Cromwell* (Owned by NRM)	4-6-2	7P5F	Great Central Railway (On loan)
71000	*Duke of Gloucester*	4-6-2	8P	Duke of Glos Locomotive Trust (owners)
73050	*City of Peterborough*	4-6-0	Std Class 5	Nene Valley Railway
73082	*Camelot*	4-6-0	Std Class 5	Bluebell Railway
73096	Was 73076	4-6-0	Std Class 5	Mid Hants Railway

Number 73076 (above) was originally restored as number 73080 and given the name *Merlin*. Later, the locomotive was renumbered 73096 and the name was removed.

NO	NAME/ OTHER INFO	WHEEL LAYOUT	CLASS	OWNER/LOCATION
73129		4-6-0	Std Class 5	Midland Railway
73156		4-6-0	Std Class 5	Great Central Railway
75014		4-6-0	Std Class 4	Dartmouth Steam Railway
75027		4-6-0	Std Class 4	Bluebell Railway
75029	*The Green Knight*	4-6-0	Std Class 4	North Yorkshire Moors Railway
75069		4-6-0	Std Class 4	Severn Valley Railway
75078		4-6-0	Std Class 4	Keighley & Worth Valley Railway
75079		4-6-0	Std Class 4	Mid Hants Railway
76017		2-6-0	Std Class 4	Mid Hants Railway

NO	NAME/ OTHER INFO	WHEEL LAYOUT	CLASS	OWNER/LOCATION
76077		2-6-0	Std Class 4	Glos Warwickshire Railway
76079		2-6-0	Std Class 4	North Yorkshire Moors Railway
76084		2-6-0	Std Class 4	North Norfolk Railway
78018		2-6-0	Std Class 2	Great Central Railway
78019		2-6-0	Std Class 2	Great Central Railway
78022		2-6-0	Std Class 2	Keighley & Worth Valley Railway
80002		2-6-4T	Std Class 4 Tank	Keighley & Worth Valley Railway
80064		2-6-4T	Std Class 4 Tank	Bluebell Railway
80072		2-6-4T	Std Class 4 Tank	Llangollen Railway
80078		2-6-4T	Std Class 4 Tank	Mangapps Railway Museum, Essex
80079		2-6-4T	Std Class 4 Tank	Severn Valley Railway
80080		2-6-4T	Std Class 4 Tank	Midland Railway
80097		2-6-4T	Std Class 4 Tank	East Lancashire Railway
80098		2-6-4T	Std Class 4 Tank	Midland Railway Centre, Butterley
80100		2-6-4T	Std Class 4 Tank	Bluebell Railway
80104		2-6-4T	Std Class 4 Tank	Swanage Railway
80105		2-6-4T	Std Class 4 Tank	Bo'ness & Kinneil Railway
80135		2-6-4T	Std Class 4 Tank	North Yorkshire Moors Railway
80136		2-6-4T	Std Class 4 Tank	North Yorkshire Moors Railway
80150		2-6-4T	Std Class 4 Tank	Mid Hants Railway
80151		2-6-4T	Std Class 4 Tank	Bluebell Railway
90733	(WD 9257)	2-10-0	8F (Austerity)	Keighley & Worth Valley Railway
90775	(WD 3652)	2-10-0	8F (Austerity)	North Norfolk Railway
Number 600	Gordon	2-10-0	8F (Austerity)	Severn Valley Railway

Number 600 (above) was built for the War Department in 1943 as WD 73651 and named after General Gordon of Khartoum. She worked on the Longmoor Military Railway, Hampshire, as number 600 until the railway closed in 1969. The locomotive was loaned to the SVR in 1971, but remained the property of the British Army who donated her to the Severn Valley Railway in 2008. She is currently on display at Highley (SVR).

NO	NAME/ OTHER INFO	WHEEL LAYOUT	CLASS	OWNER/LOCATION
92134		2-10-0	Class 9F	North Yorkshire Moors Railway
92203*	Black Prince (Named in 1968)	2-10-0	Class 9F	North Norfolk Railway
92207	Morning Star (Named in the 1980s)	2-10-0	Class 9F	Being restored at a private site in Dorset
92212		2-10-0	Class 9F	Mid Hants Railway
92214		2-10-0	Class 9F	Great Central Railway
92219		2-10-0	Class 9F	Wensleydale Railway
92220*	Evening Star (Owned by NRM)	2-10-0	Class 9F	National Railway Museum, York (on display)
92240		2-10-0	Class 9F	Bluebell Railway
92245		2-10-0	Class 9F	Barry Island Railway (South Wales)

Early British Railway Locomotives

NAME	OTHER INFORMATION	WHEEL LAYOUT	OWNER/LOCATION
Agenoria	Colliery Locomotive (Built 1829)	0-4-0	National Railway Museum, York
Billy	Colliery Locomotive (Built c. 1816–826)	0-4-0	Stephenson Museum, North Shields
Derwent	(No. 25, SDR) (Built 1845)	0-6-0	Owned by NRM. Displayed at Darlington
Hetton Colliery Locomotive	(Built c. 1822)	0-4-0	National Railway Museum, York
Invicta	(Built 1829) (C & WR)	0-4-0	Canterbury Heritage Museum
Lion	(Built 1837) (L & MR Locomotive No. 37)	0-4-2	Liverpool Museum
Locomotion No1	(Built 1825) (SDR)	0-4-0	Owned by NRM. Displayed at Darlington
Novelty	(Built in 1829 for the Rainhill Trials)	0-2-2WT	Owned by NRM. Displayed at Manchester
Puffing Billy	Colliery Locomotive (Built 1813)	0-4-0	National Railway Museum, York
Rocket	(Built in 1829 for the Rainhill Trials)	0-2-2	National Railway Museum, York
Sans Pareil	(Built in 1829 for the Rainhill Trials)	0-4-0	Owned by NRM. Displayed at Shildon
Wylam Dilly	Colliery locomotive (built 1815)	0-4-0	Royal Scottish Museum, Edinburgh
NER Locomotive No1275	(Built in 1874)	0-6-0	National Railway Museum, York

All the preserved steam locomotives listed in this book are BR Standard Gauge Locomotives (4 feet 8½ inches or 1,435 millimetres) The list does not include narrow gauge locomotives, broad gauge locomotives or industrial locomotives. New build locomotives are not listed but some individual new build locomotives are referred to.

ABOUT THE AUTHOR

After leaving school, Malcolm Clegg joined the British Transport Police for a career which lasted for almost thirty years. He served in uniform and in CID, working mainly in South Wales, policing the railway network. He did however work for a number of years as a Docks Constable at Cardiff and Newport Docks, and later as a Uniform Sergeant at Swansea and Port Talbot Docks. Almost a decade of his career was spent working at various locations in London.

The last ten years of his service were spent working as a Detective Sergeant at Swansea, covering an extensive area of south, and west Wales which included Fishguard Harbour, incorporating the then, Sealink, passenger ferry services which operated between Fishguard and Rosslare in Ireland.

After his retirement in 1992, he became an active member of the British Transport Police History Group (www.btphg.or.uk). He has carried out extensive research on behalf of the group and has written a number of articles. He is also the author of a book entitled *Nineteenth Century Railway Crime and Policing* which was published in 2017.

INDEX SECTION OF THE BOOK

Index of Photographs-Locomotive Numbers.
Book Index; British Steam Locomotives Before Preservation.

Index of Photographs-Locomotive Names.